Gilles Deleuze

An Apprenticeship in Philosophy

Michael Hardt

University of Minnesota Press
Minneapolis
London

Published by the University of Minnesota Press
2037 University Avenue Southeast, Minneapolis, MN 55455-3092
Printed in the United States of America on acid-free paper

Library of Congress Cataloging-in-Publication Data

Hardt, Michael.
   Gilles Deleuze : an apprenticeship in philosophy / Michael Hardt.
      p.   cm.
   Includes bibliographical references and index.
   ISBN 0-8166-2160-8 (acid-free).—ISBN 0-8166-2161-6 (pbk. : acid-free)
   1. Deleuze, Gilles. I. Title.
B2430.D454H37   1993
194—dc20   92-21849
                                                                      CIP

The University of Minnesota is an
equal-opportunity educator and employer.

Contents

Acknowledgments

I would like to acknowledge, with respect and affection, two of my teachers, Charles Altieri and Antonio Negri.

Hegel and the Foundations of Poststructuralism

Continental poststructuralism has problematized the foundations of philosophical and political thought. Perhaps dazzled by the impact of this theoretical rupture, diverse American authors have embraced this movement as the inauguration of a postphilosophical culture where philosophical claims and political judgments admit no justification and rest on no foundation. This problematic, however, settles too easily into a new opposition that obscures the real possibilities afforded by contemporary Continental theory. At the hands of both its supporters and its detractors, poststructuralism has been incorporated into a series of Anglo-American debates — between modernists and postmodernists, between communitarians and liberals — in such a way as to misdirect and blunt its force. The importance of poststructuralism cannot be captured by posing a new series of oppositions, but only by recognizing the nuances and alternatives it proposes within modernity, within the philosophical tradition, within the contemporary field of social practices. If we look closely at the historical development of poststructuralist thought, at the complex social and theoretical pressures it encountered and the tools it constructed to face them, we can recapture some of its critical and constructive powers. Poststructuralism, we find, is not oriented simply toward the negation of theoretical foundations, but rather toward the exploration of new grounds for philosophical and political inquiry; it is involved not simply in the rejection of the tradition of political and philosophical discourse, but more importantly in the articulation and affirmation of alternative lineages that arise from within the tradition itself.

The roots of poststructuralism and its unifying basis lie, in large part, in a general opposition not to the philosophical tradition *tout court* but specifically to the Hegelian tradition. For the generation of Continental thinkers that came to maturity in the 1960s, Hegel was the figure of order and authority that served as the focus of antagonism. Deleuze speaks for his entire cohort: "What I detested above all was Hegelianism and the dialectic" ("Lettre à Michel Cressole" 110). In order to appreciate this antagonism, however, we must realize that, in the domain of Continental theory during this period, Hegel was ubiquitous. As a result of influential interpretations by theorists as diverse as Kojève, Gramsci, Sartre, and Bobbio, Hegel had come to dominate the theoretical horizon as the ineluctable centerpiece of philosophical speculation, social theory, and political practice. In 1968, it appeared to François Châtelet that every philosopher had to begin with Hegel: "[Hegel] determined a horizon, a language, a code that we are still at the very heart of today. Hegel, by this fact, is *our* Plato: the one who delimits — ideologically or scientifically, positively or negatively — the theoretical possibilities of theory" (*Hegel* 2). Any account of Continental poststructuralism must take this framework of generalized Hegelianism as its point of departure.

The first problem of poststructuralism, then, is how to evade a Hegelian foundation. In order to understand the extent of this problem, however, we have to recognize the serious restrictions facing such a project in the specific social and historical context. Châtelet argues, in curiously dialectical fashion, that the only viable project to counter Hegelianism is to make Hegel the negative foundation of philosophy. Those who neglect the initial step of addressing and actively rejecting Hegel, he claims, those who attempt simply to turn their backs on Hegel, run the risk of ending up as mere repetitions of the Hegelian problematic. "Certainly, there are many contemporary philosophical projects that ignore Hegelianism. . . . They are dealing with the false meaning of absolute beginnings, and, moreover, they deprive themselves of a good point of support. It is better — like Marx and Nietzsche — to begin with Hegel than to end up with him" (4). Hegelianism was such a powerful vortex that in attempting to ignore it one would inevitably be sucked in by its power. Only anti-Hegelianism provided the negative point of support necessary for a post-Hegelian or even a non-Hegelian project.

From this point of view, the early works of Gilles Deleuze are exemplary of the entire generation of poststructuralist thinkers. In his early investigations into the history of philosophy we can see an intense concentration of the generalized anti-Hegelianism of the time. Deleuze attempted to confront Hegel and dialectical thought head-on, as Châtelet said one must, with a rigorous philosophical refutation; he engaged Hegelianism not in order to salvage its worthwhile elements, not to extract "the rational kernel from the mystical shell," but rather to articulate a total critique and a rejection of the negative dialectical framework so as to achieve a real autonomy, a theoretical separation from the entire Hegelian problematic. The philosophers that Deleuze selects as partisans in this struggle (Bergson, Nietzsche, and Spinoza) appear to allow him successive steps toward the realization of this project. Many recent critics of French poststructuralism, however, have charged that the poststructuralists did not understand Hegel and, with a facile anti-Hegelianism, missed the most powerful thrust of his thought.[1] Deleuze is the most important example to consider in this regard because he mounts the most focused and precise attack on Hegelianism. Nonetheless, perhaps since this cultural and philosophical paradigm was so tenacious, the attempted deracination from the Hegelian terrain is not immediately successful. We find that Deleuze often poses his project not only in the traditional language of Hegelianism but also in terms of typical Hegelian problems—the determination of being, the unity of the One and the Multiple, and so on. Paradoxically, in his effort to establish Hegel as a negative foundation for his thought, Deleuze may appear to be very Hegelian.

If Hegelianism is the first problem of poststructuralism, then, anti-Hegelianism quickly presents itself as the second. In many respects, Hegelianism is the most difficult of adversaries because it possesses such an extraordinary capacity to recuperate opposition. Many Anglo-American authors, seeking to discount the rupture of Continental poststructuralism, have rightly emphasized this dilemma. Judith Butler presents the challenge for anti-Hegelians in very clear terms: "References to a 'break' with Hegel are almost always impossible, if only because Hegel has made the very notion of 'breaking with' into the central tenet of his dialectic" (*Subjects of Desire* 184). It may seem, then, from this perspective, that to be anti-Hegelian, through a dialectical twist, becomes a position more Hegelian than ever; in effect, one might claim that the effort to be an "other" to Hegel can always be folded into an "other" within Hegel. There is in fact a growing literature that extends this line of argument, claiming that the work of contemporary anti-Hegelians consists merely in unconscious repetitions of Hegelian dramas without the power of the Hegelian subject and the rigor and clarity of the Hegelian logic.[2]

The problem of recuperation that faces the anti-Hegelian foundation of poststructuralism offers a second and more important explanation for our selection of Deleuze in this study. Although numerous authors have made important contributions to our critique of Hegel, Deleuze has gone the furthest in extricating himself from the problems of anti-Hegelianism and constructing an alternative terrain for thought—no longer post-Hegelian but rather separate from the problem of Hegel. If our first reason for proposing Deleuze as an exemplary poststructuralist thinker was that he is representative of the antagonism to Hegelianism, our second is that he is anomalous in his extension of that project away from Hegel toward a separate, alternative terrain. There are two central elements of this passage that Deleuze develops in different registers and on different planes of thought: a nondialectical conception of negation and a constitutive theory of practice. We cannot understand these elements, I repeat, if we merely oppose them to Hegelian conceptions of negation and practice. We must recognize their nuances and pose them on an alternative plane. These two themes, then, negation and practice, understood with their new forms, comprise the foundation of the new terrain that poststructuralism has to offer for philosophical and political thought, a terrain for contemporary research.

Let us briefly examine the general outlines of these two central elements of Deleuze's project. The concept of negation that lies at the center of dialectical thought seems to pose the most serious challenge for any theory that claims to be anti- or post-Hegelian. "Nondialectical difference," Judith Butler writes, "despite its various forms, is the labor of the negative which has lost its 'magic' " (184). The nondialectical concept of negation that we find in Deleuze's total critique certainly contains none of the magical effect of the dialectic. The dialectical negation is always directed toward the miracle of resurrection: It is a negation "which supersedes in such a way as to preserve and maintain what is superseded, and consequently survives its own supersession" (*Phenomenology of Spirit* §188). Nondialectical negation is more simple and more absolute. With no faith in the beyond, in the eventual resurrection, negation becomes an extreme moment of nihilism: In Hegelian terms, it points to the death of the other. Hegel considers this pure death, "the absolute Lord," merely an abstract conception of negation; in the contemporary world, however, the absolute character of negation has become dreadfully concrete, and the magical resurrection implicit in the dialectical negation appears merely as superstition. Nondialectical negation is absolute not in the sense that everything present is negated but in that what is negated is attacked with full, unrestrained force. On the one hand, authors like Deleuze propose this nondialectical concept of negation not in the promotion of nihilism, but merely as the recognition of an element of our world. We can situate this theoretical position in relation to the field of "nuclear criticism," but not in the sense that nuclear weapons pose the threat of negation, not in the sense that they pose the universal fear of death: This is merely the "standing negation" of a Hegelian framework, preserving the given order. The negation of the bomb is nondialectical in its actuality, not in the planning rooms of Washington but in the streets of Hiroshima, as an agent of total destruction. There is nothing positive in the nondialectical negation, no magical resurrection: It is pure. On the other hand, with an eye toward the philosophical tradition, we can locate this radical conception of negation in the methodological proposals of certain Scholastic authors such as Roger Bacon. The pure negation is the first moment of a precritical conception of critique: *pars destruens, pars construens*. The important characteristics are the purity and autonomy of the two critical moments. Negation clears the terrain for creation; it is a bipartite sequence that precludes any third, synthetic moment. Thus we can at least gesture toward solid grounds for this radical, nondialectical negation: It is as new as the destructive force of contemporary warfare and as old as the precritical skepticism of the Scholastics.

The radicality of negation forces Deleuze to engage questions of the lowest order, questions of the nature of being. Deleuze's total critique involves a destruction so absolute that it becomes necessary to question what makes reality possible. We should emphasize that, on one hand, the rejection of Hegelian ontology does not lead Deleuze to some form of de-ontological thought. Although he denies any preconstituted structure of being or any teleological order of existence, Deleuze still operates on the highest planes of ontological speculation. Once again, to reject Hegelian ontology is not to reject ontology *tout court*. Deleuze insists instead on alternatives within the ontological tradition. On the other hand, however, we should be careful from the outset to distinguish this from a Heideggerian return to ontology, most importantly because Deleuze will only accept "superficial" responses to the question "What makes being possible?" In other words, he limits us to a strictly immanent and materialist ontological discourse that refuses any deep or hidden foundation of being. There is nothing veiled or negative about Deleuze's being; it is fully expressed in the world. Being, in this sense, is superficial, positive, and full. Deleuze refuses any "intellectualist" account of being, any account that in any way subordinates being to thought, that poses thinking as the supreme form of being.[3] There are numerous contributions to this project of a materialist ontology throughout the history of philosophy—such as Spinoza, Marx, Nietzsche, and Lucretius—and we will refer to them in our discussion to provide illustrative points of reference. We will focus, however, on Deleuze's constitutive conception of practice as a foundation of ontology. The radical negation of the nondialectical *pars destruens* emphasizes that no preconstituted order is available to define the organization of being. Practice provides the terms for a material *pars construens*; practice is what makes the constitution of being possible. The investigation of the nature of power allows Deleuze to bring substance to the materialist discourse and to raise the theory of practice to the level of ontology. The foundation of being, then, resides both on a corporeal and on a mental plane, in the complex dynamics of behavior, in the superficial interactions of bodies. This is not an Althusserian "theoretical practice," but rather a more practical conception of practice, autonomous of any "theoricist tendency," a "practical practice" that is oriented principally toward the ontological rather than the epistemological realm. The only nature available to ontological discourse is an absolutely artificial conception of nature, a hybrid nature, a nature produced in practice—further removed than a second nature, an nth nature. This approach to ontology is as new as the infinitely plastic universe of cyborgs and as old as the tradition of materialist philosophy. What will be important throughout our discussion is that the traditionally fundamental terms—such as necessity, reason, nature, and being—though shaken from their transcendental fixity, still serve as a foundation because they acquire a certain consistency and substance in our world. Being, now historicized and materialized, is delimited by the outer bounds of the contemporary imagination, of the contemporary field of practice.

I elaborate these conceptions of nondialectical negation and constitutive practice in Deleuze's work by reading the evolution of his thought, that is, by following the progression of critical questions that guide his investigations during successive periods. The evolution of Deleuze's thought unfolds as he directs his attention sequentially to a series of authors in the philosophical canon and poses them each a specific question. His work on Bergson offers a critique of negative ontology and proposes in its stead an absolutely positive movement of being that rests on an efficient and internal notion of causality. To the negative movement of determination, he opposes the positive movement of differentiation; to the dialectical unity of the One and the Multiple, he opposes the irreducible multiplicity of becoming. The question of the organization or the constitution of the world, however, of the being of becoming, pushes Deleuze to pose these ontological issues in ethical terms. Nietzsche allows him to transpose the results of ontological speculation to an ethical horizon, to the field of forces, of sense and value, where the positive movement of being becomes the affirmation of being. The thematic of power in Nietzsche provides the theoretical passage that links Bergsonian ontology to an ethics of active expression. Spinoza covers this same passage and extends it to practice. Just as Nietzsche poses the affirmation of speculation, Spinoza poses the affirmation of practice, or joy, at the center of ontology. Deleuze argues that Spinoza's is an ontological conception of practice; Spinoza conceives practice, that is, as constitutive of being. In the precritical world of Spinoza's practical philosophy, Deleuze's thought finally discovers a real autonomy from the Hegelian problematic.

One lesson to be learned from this philosophical project is to highlight the nuances that define an antagonism. Once we stop clouding the issue with crude oppositions and recognize instead the specificity of an antagonism, we can begin to bring out finer nuances in our terminology. For example, when I pose the question of the *foundations* of poststructuralist thought I mean to contest the claim that this thought is properly characterized as antifoundationalism. To pose the issue as an exclusive opposition is, in effect, to credit the enemy with too much force, with too much theoretical terrain. Poststructuralism does critique a certain notion of foundation, but only to affirm another notion that is more adequate to its ends. Against a transcendental foundation we find an immanent one; against a given, teleological foundation we find a material, open one.[4] A similar nuance must be made in our discussion of causality. When we look closely at Deleuze's critique of causality we find not only a powerful rejection of the final cause and the formal cause, but also an equally powerful affirmation of the efficient cause as central to his philosophical project. Deleuze's ontology draws on the tradition of causal arguments and develops notions of both being's "productivity" and its "producibility," that is, of its aptitudes to produce and to be produced. I will argue that efficient causality, in fact, provides a key to a coherent account of Deleuze's entire discourse on difference. The nuances in the use of "foundation" and "causality" are perhaps best summarized by the distinction between order and organization. By the order of being, of truth, or of society I intend the structure imposed as necessary and eternal from above, from outside the material scene of forces; I use organization, on the other hand, to designate the coordination and accumulation of accidental (in the philosophical sense, i.e., nonnecessary) encounters and developments from below, from within the immanent field of forces. In other words, I do not conceive of organization as a blueprint of development or as the projected vision of an avant-garde, but rather as an immanent creation or composition of a relationship of consistency and coordination. In this sense, organization, the composition of creative forces, is always an art.

Throughout this study we will encounter unresolved problems and propositions that are powerfully suggestive but perhaps not clearly and rigorously delimited. We do not look to Deleuze here, however, simply to find the solutions to contemporary theoretical problems. More important, we inquire into his thought in order to investigate the proposals of a new problematic for research after the poststructuralist rupture, to test our footing on a terrain where new grounds of philosophical and political thought are possible. What we ask of Deleuze, above all, is to teach us the contemporary possibilities of philosophy.

The Early Deleuze: Some Methodological Principles

In the Introduction to *Instincts et institutions*, a collection of texts edited by Deleuze in 1953, we see the general outlines of a philosophical and political project beginning to take shape as a theory of the institution. "Contrary to the theories of law that put the positive outside of the social (natural rights) and the social in the negative (contractual limitation), the theory of the institution puts the negative outside of the social (needs) in order to present society as essentially positive and inventive (original means of satisfaction)" (ix). This schematic presentation of a theory of the institution already gives us two fundamental elements of Deleuze's project: It designates the attack on "the negative" as a political task and it poses the central productive object of philosophy as the construction of a purely positive, inventive society. We can already recognize latent here a powerful notion of constitution and a suggestive glimpse of a radically democratic theory. Admittedly, though, at this early point Deleuze's use of "the negative" and "the positive" is rather vague and thus the proposition can only provide an initial intuition of a project. One could attempt to read Deleuze's book on Hume, *Empiricism and Subjectivity*, with its focus on association and belief, as an early attempt to address directly this politicophilosophical project.[1] However, the general development of Deleuze's thought does not immediately follow this line; it becomes clear that Deleuze requires an extensive ontological detour before arriving at this positive political project. There is not the space nor the terms for this constructive project without first conducting a broad destructive operation. Deleuze's early work thus always takes the form of a critique: *pars destruens, pars construens*. Throughout this period, the cutting edge of Deleuze's thought is a persistent, implacable siege on Hegelianism, an attack on the negative. Even in his very first published article, "Du Christ à la bourgeoisie," published when he was only twenty-one years old, we can already recognize anti-Hegelianism as a driving force of his thought: What characterizes Hegel better, after all, than the strict continuity between Christianity and bourgeois thought? It is important to establish and clarify the terms of this antagonism from the outset in order to gain a clear perspective on the sense and trajectory of Deleuze's overall project. The various *mots d'ordre* heralded by Deleuze in this period—the destruction of the negative, the affirmation of the positive—lack their full power and significance when they are not firmly grounded in an antagonistic engagement of Hegel. As Deleuze himself asserts while reading Nietzsche, in order to gain an adequate understanding of a philosophical project one must recognize against whom its principal concepts are directed (*Nietzsche and Philosophy* 8, 162). This, then, constitutes our first methodological principle for reading Deleuze: *Recognize the object and the terms of the primary antagonism.*

Deleuze's detour, though, is not only an attack but also the establishment of new terrain: The early intuition of a positive political project is recast by means of the long passage that we will follow—from Bergson to Nietzsche and finally to Spinoza. Deleuze requires a positive ontology in order to establish a positive theory of ethics and social organization. This long passage through the history of Western philosophy forges a multifarious edifice on the highest planes of metaphysical meditation that supports and informs the entire breadth of Deleuze's work. One can certainly recognize, even in the early works, a desire to move away from philosophy, to depart from his training and branch out into other fields: biology, psychology, art, mathematics, politics, literature. Many read Deleuze's work as a rejection of Western philosophical thought and hence the proposition of a postphilosophical or postmodern discourse. Indeed, Deleuze himself provides numerous statements to substantiate such an interpretation.[2] However, when we look closely at his arguments, we find that not only is his thought saturated with the Western philosophical tradition, but even when his examples seem "unphilosophical" the coherence of his positions and the mode of explanation that supports them remain on the highest logical and ontological planes.[3] If, then, we are to read Deleuze's work as an attack or betrayal of elements of the Western metaphysical tradition, we have to understand this as an affirmation of other elements of that same tradition. In other words, we cannot read Deleuze's work as thought "outside" or "beyond" the philosophical tradition, or even as an effective line of flight from that block; rather we must see it as the affirmation of a (discontinuous, but coherent) line of thought that has remained suppressed and dormant, but nonetheless deeply embedded within that same tradition. Deleuze does not announce the end of metaphysics, but on the contrary seeks to rediscover the most coherent and lucid plane of metaphysical thought.[4] If we wanted to insist on his rejection of a certain form of philosophical inquiry, we would have to pose the statement in paradoxical form and say (borrowing a phrase from Althusser) that Deleuze develops "a nonphilosophical theory of philosophy." In any case, if in the course of this study our references to the resonances between Deleuze's work and other positions in the philosophical tradition seem at times excessive, it is precisely to emphasize the properly philosophical nature of his thought. Here, then, we have our second methodological principle: *Read Deleuze philosophically.*

Deleuze's journey through the history of philosophy takes a peculiar form. Even though Deleuze's monographs serve as excellent introductions, they never provide a comprehensive summary of a philosopher's work; instead, Deleuze selects the specific aspects of a philosopher's thought that make a positive contribution to his own project at that point. As Nietzschean or as Spinozist, Deleuze does not accept all of Nietzsche or all of Spinoza. If a philosopher presents arguments with which Deleuze might find fault, he does not critique them but simply leaves them out of his discussion. Might it be said, then, that Deleuze is an unfaithful reader? Certainly not. If his readings are partial, they are nonetheless very rigorous and precise, with meticulous care and sensitivity to the selected topics; what Deleuze forfeits in comprehensiveness, he gains in intensity of focus. In effect, Deleuze's early works are "punctual interventions"—he makes surgical incisions in the corpus of the history of philosophy. This leads us to our third methodological principle: *Recognize Deleuze's selectivity.*

In each of the stages of this philosophical journey, Deleuze adds a specific point that builds and depends on the previous results. Each of Deleuze's philosophical monographs is directed toward a very specific question, and viewed as an ensemble the development of these philosophical questions reveals the evolution of Deleuze's thought. Often, Deleuze's explanations appear incomplete because he takes for granted and fails to repeat the results of his previous research. (For example, as we will see below, many of Deleuze's claims for Nietzsche's attack on the dialectic remain obscure unless we read into them a Bergsonian critique of a negative ontological movement.) Therefore, Deleuze's early work constructs an odd sort of history of philosophy in which the connecting links depend not on actual philosophical historiography but on the evolution of Deleuze's own thought. By evolution I do not mean to suggest a unilinear or teleological progression, but rather a sort of theoretical process of aggregation.

Focusing on this progression highlights the movement in Deleuze's thought, and what emerges is the process of Deleuze's own philosophical education, his apprenticeship in philosophy. The lines of this educational journey help explain the counterhistorical development Bergson-Nietzsche-Spinoza that guides Deleuze from ontology to ethics and politics.[5] Hence, we can posit a final methodological principle: *Read Deleuze's thought as an evolution*.

When we look at Deleuze's early work from a historical perspective, as an evolution, the most striking fact is that he wrote his first book when he was rather young (he was twenty-eight years old in 1953 when *Empiricism and Subjectivity* appeared) and then waited eight years before publishing his next book. Eight years might not seem like a very long break for some authors, but for Deleuze, who after 1962 consistently published a book each year, eight years represents an enormous gap. "It's like a hole in my life, an eight-year hole. That is what I find interesting in lives, the holes they have, the lacunas, sometimes dramatic, sometimes not. . . . Perhaps it is in the holes that the movement takes place" ("Signes et événements" 18). This eight-year hole in Deleuze's intellectual life does in fact represent a period of movement, a dramatic reorientation of his philosophical approach. During this period, in effect, he shifts from the Hume-Bergson axis that characterizes his very early work to the Nietzsche-Spinoza identity that carries his work to its maturity. In order to read this hole in Deleuze's intellectual life, we must try to interpret what this reorientation can mean, what new possibilities it affords Deleuze, and how it characterizes the evolution of his thought.

This focus on the evolution of Deleuze's philosophical education best explains why I have chosen in the following study to deal exclusively with his early writings. In these works Deleuze develops a technical vocabulary and conceptual foundation that serve him through the entire trajectory of his career. The positions of the later works can appear obscure, even untenable, when we do not place them in the context of these early investigations. Indeed, some of the most spectacular innovations in what one might call his mature work—the major independent philosophical texts (*Différence et répétition* and *The Logic of Sense*), the collaborations with Félix Guattari, the cinema studies, and the latest works—are in large part reworkings of the cluster of problems developed in this formative period of intense and independent research. The profound originality of Deleuze's voice is perhaps due to the fact that during these years he was not following the same course as the majority of his generation.[6] This is the period of Deleuze's subterranean research—the period in which he forged new paths, outside of the limelight and commonplaces of public French cultural debates—that perhaps allowed him to surface with such a profound impact later. If, in fact, as Michel Foucault suspected, this difference does come to mark our century, if our times do become Deleuzian, this early work, the subterranean Deleuze, will hold the key to the formative developments that made this new paradigm possible.

Chapter 1

Bergsonian Ontology
The Positive Movement of Being

In the work of Henri Bergson, one might expect to find a psychology or a phenomenology of perception. It may seem strange at first, then, that what Deleuze finds principally is an ontology: an absolutely positive logic of being rooted in time. As we have noted, though, Deleuze does not move directly to the positive project but rather approaches first by means of a critical, aggressive moment: "What Bergson essentially reproaches his predecessors for. . . . " ("La conception de la différence chez Bergson" 79). Deleuze reads Bergson as a polemic against the dominant philosophical tradition, and the faults of his predecessors are found in their most concentrated form in Hegel's logic; Bergson critiques several philosophical arguments, but behind each of these Deleuze finds Hegel occupying an extreme, exaggerated position. Deleuze does not claim that a direct antagonism against Hegel is what primarily drives Bergson's thought, but his reading of Bergson continually retains the attack on Hegel as its own critical edge. In Deleuze's interpretation, Bergson does not challenge the central criteria for being inherited from the ontological tradition— simplicity, reality, perfection, unity, multiplicity, and so on—but rather he focuses on the ontological movement that is posed to address these criteria. "Difference" is the Bergsonian term that plays the central role in this discussion of ontological movement. We should be especially attentive at this point, because Deleuze's interpretation of Bergson (formulated as early as 1956) stands at the head of a long discourse on difference in French thought that constitutes a theoretical touchstone for poststructural-

1

ism. Here we find a particular and rigorous usage of the term. In Deleuze's reading, Bergson's difference does not principally refer to a quidditas or to a static contrast of qualities in real being; rather, difference marks the real dynamic of being—it is the movement that grounds being. Thus, Bergson's difference relates primarily to the temporal, not the spatial, dimension of being. The essential task that Deleuze sets for himself in the investigation of Bergson's concept of difference, then, is twofold. First, he must use Bergson's critique of the ontological tradition to reveal the weakness of Hegel's dialectic and its negative logic of being, as a false conception of difference. This attack is directed against two foundational moments of Hegel's logic: the determination of being and the dialectic of the One and the Multiple. Second, he must elaborate Bergson's positive movement of being in difference and show how this movement provides a viable alternative for ontology. It is precisely the aggressive moment against Hegelian logic that prepares the ground for the productive moment.

Deleuze's work on Bergson, however, presents a complication—and at the same time an opportunity—for studying the evolution of his thought because it is conducted in two distinct periods: one in the mid-1950s and another in the mid-1960s. The major result of the first period is an article titled "La conception de la différence chez Bergson," which was published in *Les études bergsoniennes* in 1956 but written at least two years earlier and presented to the "Association des amies de Bergson" in May 1954. This early article is very dense and contains the major points of Deleuze's reading of Bergson. Deleuze published two other Bergson texts in this period, but neither substantially modifies the early essay. The first is a chapter on Bergson for a collection edited by Merleau-Ponty, *Les philosophes célèbres* (1956), and the second is a selection of Bergson texts, *Mémoire et vie* (1957). The result of Deleuze's second period of Bergson study is *Bergsonism*, published in 1966. This short book takes up much of the argument presented in the early article but shows a change in focus and offers some very interesting additions to the original interpretation, additions that show the influence of Deleuze's intense Nietzsche period in the intervening years. These two phases of Bergson study, then, provide an excellent opportunity to read the orientation of Deleuze's early project, because they straddle not only the work on Nietzsche (1962) but also the long publication gap, the "eight-year hole" that, as Deleuze suggests, may be a site of considerable reorientation of the project.

1.1 Determination and Efficient Difference

Deleuze's early reading of Bergson is grounded on an attack against the negative process of determination. The specter that looms over this ques-

tion throughout Modern philosophy is Hegel's reading and critique of
Spinoza. Hegel takes a phrase from one of Spinoza's letters and, turning it
back against Spinoza, makes it a central maxim of his own logic: "Omnis
determinatio est negatio" (*Science of Logic* 113).[1] This phrase describes for
Hegel the process of determination and the state of determinateness. The
Logic begins with pure being in its simple immediacy; but this simple being has no quality, no difference—it is empty and equivalent to its opposite, nothingness. It is necessary that being actively negate nothingness to
mark its difference from it. Determinate being subsumes this opposition,
and this difference between being and nothingness at its core defines the
foundation of the real differences and qualities that constitute its reality.
Negation defines this state of determinateness in two senses: It is a static
contrast based on the finitude of qualities and a dynamic *conflict* based on
the antagonism of differences (see Taylor 233-37). In the first sense, determinateness involves negation because qualities are limited and thus contrast, or passively negate, what is other than themselves (in the sense that
red negates green, yellow, etc.). In the second sense, however, there is an
active negation that animates determinateness, because determinate things
are in a causal interaction with each other. The existence of something is
the active negation of something else. Therefore, even the *state* of determinateness is essentially a negative *movement*. This insistence on a negative movement of determination is also the heart of Hegel's critique of
Spinoza. Since Spinoza's being is absolutely positive, in other words since
in Spinoza pure being does not actively negate nothingness and does not
proceed through a negative movement, it lacks the fundamental difference
that could define its real existence. In Hegel's eyes, Spinoza's ontology and
any such positive, affirmative ontology must remain abstract and indifferent. "Reality as thus conceived [as perfection and affirmation] is assumed to
survive when all negation has been thought away; but to do this is to do
away with all determinateness" (*Science of Logic* 112). Negation cannot
merely be passively "thought away," Hegel maintains, but must be actively
engaged and really negated—this is the role of the process of determination. Consequently, finally, inevitably, because Spinoza's being is not held
different from nothingness as its opposite, it dissolves into nothingness just
as does Spinoza himself in Hegel's Romantic imagination: "The cause of
his death was consumption, from which he had long been a sufferer; this
was in harmony with his system of philosophy, according to which all particularity and individuality pass away in the one substance" (*Lectures on the
History of Philosophy* 257). This polemic against Spinoza constitutes one of
Hegel's strongest arguments for the ontological movement of negation:
Being not determined through negation will remain indifferent and abstract, and finally, since it is not held different from its opposite, it will fade

into nothingness. Hegel insists that if we are to recognize difference, the real difference that characterizes the particularity and individuality of being, we must first recognize the negative movement of being; or else, we must disappear along with Spinoza in "acosmism," in the indifference of pure, positive ontology.

Deleuze's early reading of Bergson seems to accept the Hegelian formulation that the determination of being must be characterized by negation. Rather than challenging that formulation, Deleuze charges that the process of ontological determination itself undermines the real grounding of being; he claims that the difference constituted by the negative movement of determination is a false notion of difference. Hence, the process of determination both destroys the substantial nature of being and fails to grasp the concreteness and specificity of real being. Here, with the rejection of determination, we can recognize the anti-Hegelian approach of Deleuze's early work, his reaction to the dialectic of negation. In this process, however, Deleuze's critical method takes on an interesting form. He does not attack the dialectic directly, but rather he introduces a third philosophical position that he locates between Bergson and the dialectic. Deleuze engages this proximate enemy on the specific fault that marks its insufficiency, and then he proceeds to show that Hegel, the fundamental enemy, carries this fault to its extreme. In the Bergson studies, Deleuze engages Mechanicism and Platonism as the proximate enemies, and in the Nietzsche study he brings in Kant. The advantage of first addressing these proximate enemies is that they provide a common ground on which to work out the attack that can be subsequently extended to the dialectic. Indeed, as Deleuze's thought evolves we will see that he has continually greater difficulty in finding a common terrain for addressing the Hegelian position. More important, though, this method of triangulation shows us that even in this early work Deleuze has a problematic relation to opposition. It is clear that Deleuze is attacking the dialectic as the fundamental enemy, but this method affords him an oblique posture with regard to Hegel so that he does not have to stand in direct opposition.

Like Bergson, the Mechanicists try to theorize an empirical evolution of the differences of being, but in doing so Mechanicism destroys the substantial, necessary quality of being. Deleuze's Bergsonian challenge to Mechanicism takes the form of a curious proposition: In order for being to be necessary, it must be indeterminate. This discussion of ontological determination turns on an analysis of the nature of difference. The form of difference proposed by the process of determination, Deleuze argues, always remains external to being and therefore fails to provide it with an essential, necessary foundation. These are the terms Deleuze uses to critique the simple determination of Mechanicism: "Bergson shows that vital difference is an *internal* difference. But also, that internal difference cannot be conceived as a simple *determination*: a determination can be accidental, at least it can only sustain its being through a cause, an end, or a chance [elle ne peut tenir son être que d'une cause, d'une fin ou d'un hasard], and it therefore implies a subsistent exteriority" ("La conception de la différence chez Bergson" 92). A Mechanistic determination of being, while it attempts to trace the evolution of reality, destroys the necessity of being. The external difference of determination is always reliant on an "other" (as cause, end, or chance) and thus it introduces an accidental quality into being; in other words, determination implies a mere subsistent exteriority, not a substantial interiority.

Right away, however, we have to find Deleuze's explanation puzzling. In effect, Deleuze has reversed the terms of the traditional ontological problematic here. He does not question how being can gain determinacy, how being can sustain its difference, but rather how difference "can sustain its being [peut tenir son être]." Deleuze gives difference a radically new role. Difference founds being; it provides being with its necessity, its substantiality. We cannot understand this argument for internal difference over external difference unless we recognize the ontologically fundamental role that difference is required to fill. I would suggest that we can best understand Deleuze's explanation through reference to Scholastic conceptions of the ontological centrality of causality and the productivity of being.[2] In many respects Deleuze reads Bergsonian ontology as a Scholasticism in which the discourse on causality is replaced with a discussion of difference.[3] We do not have to depart very far from the text to read the claim that determination "can only sustain its being through a cause, an end, or a chance" as an attack on three conceptions of causality that are inadequate for the foundation of being: (1) material—a purely physical cause that gives rise to an external effect; (2) final—a cause that refers to the end or goal in the production of its effect; (3) accidental—a cause that has a completely contingent relation to its effect. What is central in each case is that the cause remains external to its effect and therefore can only sustain the *possibility* of being. For being to be necessary, the fundamental ontological cause must be internal to its effect. This internal cause is the efficient cause that plays the central role in Scholastic ontological foundations. Furthermore, it is only the efficient cause, precisely because of its internal nature, that can sustain being as substance, as *causa sui*.[4] In the Bergsonian context, then, we might say that efficient difference is the difference that is the internal motor of being: It sustains being's necessity and real substantiality. Through this internal productive dynamic, the being of efficient difference is *causa sui*. The determination of Mechanism cannot fill this role because it is constituted by an external, material causality. We should emphasize here that Deleuze's argument is certainly not a critique of causality *tout court*, but rather a rejection of external conceptions of cause in favor of an internal, efficient notion.

After having laid out the terms of an attack on the external difference of determination with the critique of Mechanicism, Deleuze engages Plato, a second proximate enemy, to refine the attack. Deleuze recognizes that Plato shares with Bergson the project to construct a philosophy of differ-ence ("La conception de la différence chez Bergson" 95), but what Deleuze challenges in Plato is the principle of finality. Once again, the cri-tique is focused on the external nature of difference with the ontological criteria as measure. In Bergson difference is driven by an internal motor (which Bergson calls intuition), whereas in Plato this role is only filled by an external inspiration from the finality: The difference of the thing can only be accounted for by its destination, the Good (95). If we translate this into causal discourse, we can say that Plato tries to found being on the final cause. Although Bergson, like Plato, does conceive of the articulations of reality in terms of functions and ends, in Bergson there is no separation between difference and the thing, between cause and effect: "The thing and the corresponding end are in fact one and the same. . . . There is no longer any room to talk about an end: When difference has become the thing itself, there is no longer room to say that the thing receives its differ-ence from an end" (96). Once again, the discussion of difference is per-fectly consistent with a causal ontological argument: Bergson's efficient dif-ference is contrasted to Plato's final difference. The key to the argument turns, as it did in the case of Mechanicism, on the need for difference to sustain a substantial nature, on its ontological centrality. Bergson presents difference as *causa sui*, supported by an internal dynamic, while Plato's difference is forced to rely on the external support of finality. Hence, Pla-tonic difference is not capable of supporting being in its substantiality and necessity.

This explanation of the faults of Mechanicism and Platonism provides us with a means of understanding the Bergsonian distinction that Deleuze finds so important between "differences of nature" and "differences of de-gree." "What Bergson essentially reproaches his predecessors for is not having seen the real differences of nature. . . . Where there were differ-ences of nature, they only recognized differences of degree" (79). At times it seems as if Deleuze and Bergson are using these terms to distinguish between qualitative and quantitative differences, but, especially given the sweeping claim about the originality of this conception in the history of philosophy, this interpretation proves inadequate. We gain a much clearer perspective if we refer, once again, to the tradition of Scholastic causal ar-guments: "Differences of nature" appear as those differences that imply necessity and substance, corresponding to the Scholastic *causae per se*; thus, "differences of degree" are those that imply accidents, *causae per accidens*.[5] "Thinking internal difference as such, as pure internal difference, arriving at a pure concept of difference, raising difference to the absolute—that is the sense of Bergson's effort" (90). While Mechanism and Platonism do succeed in thinking difference, they only arrive at contingent differences (*per accidens*); Bergson's conception of internal difference leads us to recognize substantial differences (*per se*).

Hegelianism, however, is the fundamental target we find at the base of each of these critiques; Hegel is the one who takes the exteriority of difference to its extreme. "One can even, based on certain of Bergson's texts, foresee the objections that he would make to a dialectic of the Hegelian type, which he is much further from than that of Plato" (96). One might expect that with the critique of Platonic finality as an introduction Deleuze would mount an attack against the final cause and teleology in Hegel—in effect, he already has the weapons for such an attack at his disposal. Instead, he turns back to the process of determination and the basic negative movement of the dialectic, to the founding moment of Hegel's logic. "In Bergson ... the thing differs with itself *first, immediately*. According to Hegel, the thing differs with itself because it differs first with all that it is not" (96). In Bergson, the thing immediately differs with itself; in other words, the difference of the thing is sustained through an internal, efficient production. The common fault of Mechanism and Platonism is that they both conceive of difference as dependent on an external support; however, they each identify specific external supports (an external material thing in Mechanism and a function or finality in Plato), and thus the exteriority of difference in each case is limited. Hegelian dialectics takes external difference to its extreme, to absolute exteriority, "all the way to contradiction." The dialectic presents the thing differing with an unlimited other, "with all that it is not"—this is absolute exteriority. In effect, if we ignore the question of historiography, Hegel appears to gather the faults of Mechanism and Platonism and repeat them in their pure form by taking external difference to its extreme.

The Bergsonian critique is obvious when we focus on the causality implied by the dialectic. From the very first moments of *Science of Logic*—from pure being to nothingness to determinate being—the dialectic is constituted by a dynamic in which the cause is absolutely external to its effect: This is the essence of a dialectic of contradiction. The process of the mediation in the opposite necessarily depends on an external causality. As such, Hegel's logic of being is vulnerable to a Scholastic response: A conception of being founded on an external cause cannot sustain the necessity or substantiality of being because a cause external to its effect cannot be necessary; the successive external mediations that found dialectical being cannot constitute *causae per se* but must rather be recognized as *causae per accidens*. Thus, because of the contingency of this external causal movement, the being of the dialectic is the extreme case of a "subsistent exteriority." The core of a Bergsonian attack on the Hegelian concept of dialectical mediation, then, is that it cannot sustain being as necessary and substantial.

Not only does the Hegelian dialectic, like Mechanicism and Platonism, introduce accident into being, but it also fails to grasp the concreteness and singularity of being: "Now, if the objection that Bergson could raise against Platonism was that it remained a conception of *difference that is still external*, the objection that he makes to a dialectic of contradictions is that it remains a conception of *difference that is only abstract*" (96-97). The logic of this further attack is not immediately clear. How does it follow that the difference of dialectical difference is abstract merely from the condition that its support is absolutely external? Deleuze backs up this claim by quoting Bergson on the logic of external perception: "It is hardly concrete reality on which one can take at the same time two opposing views, and subsume consequently the two antagonistic concepts. . . . This combination (of two contradictory concepts) cannot present either a diversity of degree or a variety of forms: It is or it is not" (96-97, cited from *La Pensée et le Mouvant* 198, 207). Once again, the argument is most clearly understood in terms of causality. First, Bergson claims that a dialectic of opposites remains a mere "combination" of two terms, not a synthesis, because the terms remain absolutely external to one another and thus cannot form a coherent, necessary causal chain. This charge is backed once again by the principle that an external cause cannot be necessary. Second, Bergson claims that the result of this combination of abstract concepts cannot produce something concrete and real. This claim is based on another fundamental principle of causality: An effect cannot contain more reality or perfection than its cause. The heart of a Bergsonian attack on the Hegelian concept of dialectical synthesis, then, is that its result must remain both contingent and abstract.

Up to this point we have considered Deleuze's Bergsonian attack on Hegel's negative ontological movement as it is presented in Deleuze's first phase of Bergson study, and mainly in the early article "La conception de la différence chez Bergson." Deleuze has attributed difference with an onto-logically foundational role and then constructed a scale for evaluating various conceptions of difference based on their capacity to fulfill this role. We have found that, because of the ontological demands at its core, Deleuze's discussion on difference can be clearly understood if it is continually referred to a Scholastic discourse on causality. Bergson's internal difference, appearing as an efficient causality, grasps differences of nature or differences that support substance in its necessity and reality; the external difference presented by the proximate enemies, Mechanicism and Platonism, is only capable of carrying differences of degree that cannot support being as necessary; finally, the Hegelian dialectic, with its absolutely external negative movement, can grasp neither differences of nature nor differences of degree—the being of the dialectic remains not only contingent but also abstract. "That which carries neither degrees nor nuances is an abstraction" (97).[6] The negative movement of dialectical determination, while purporting to establish the basis for real difference, actually ignores difference altogether. Deleuze has managed to turn Hegel's argument for determination completely upside down. Hegel proposes the negative movement of determination on the basis of the charge that Spinoza's positive movement remains abstract and indifferent; here, however, on the basis of classic ontological argumentation, Deleuze turns the charge of abstraction against Hegel and claims that dialectical determination ignores difference: "One has substituted for difference the game of determination" (96). The antagonistic project against Hegel is clearly the driving force of this argument. When Deleuze claims that "not only is vital difference not a determination, but it is rather the contrary—given the choice it would be indetermination itself" (92), it is very clear "against whom" these concepts are directed. Indeed, the acceptance of the term "indetermination" to describe Bergson's difference should be read principally as a refutation of the negative movement of the dialectic. We should note here that this early article is the only occasion on which Deleuze attacks the Hegelian dialectic directly, on its own terms, and perhaps for this reason it is his most powerful critique. Later, when Deleuze returns to attack the dialectic in the second Bergson phase of study, in his work on Nietzsche or in *Différence et répétition*, he always addresses an extrapolation or derivation of the dialectic.

This direct antagonistic foundation, however, already raises a serious problem: The radical opposition to the dialectic appears to force us to read Bergsonian being as "indeterminate" in the Hegelian sense. We will find later, however, that Hegel's claims about the attributes of the state of determinate being—quality, finitude, and reality—are equally claimed by the being of Bergson's internal difference.[7] Deleuze feels the need to correct this false impression, warning us not to confuse Bergsonian "indetermination" with irrationality or abstraction: "When [Bergson] talks about determination he does not invite us to abandon reason, but to arrive at the true reason of the thing in the process of making itself, the philosophical reason that is not determination but difference" ("Bergson" 299). We will find, in fact, that Bergson's "indetermination" has little to do with Hegel's "determination," but rather it relates to an idea of the creativity and originality of real being: "*l'imprévisible*," the unforeseeable. Bergson's term is neither consistent with nor opposite to Hegel's. We will return to the specifics of Bergson's positive ontology; it is sufficient at this point to recognize the force and the initial consequences of the antagonistic foundation of Deleuze's argument.

1.2 Multiplicity in the Passage from Quality to Quantity

When Deleuze returns to Bergson in the mid-1960s to write *Bergsonism*, he takes up again many of his early arguments, but his polemical foundation changes slightly. The analysis still contains an attack against the negative movement of determination, but now the central critical focus is directed toward the problem of the One and the Multiple. This reorientation, however, does not by any means mark a departure from the earlier analysis, but simply a progression: We can imagine that Deleuze has merely continued in his reading of "The Doctrine of Being" in Hegel's *Science of Logic*, moving from chapter 2 on determinate being to chapter 3 on the construction of being-for-self through the dialectical relationship of the One and the Multiple. It is still the opposition to Hegel's ontological problematic that provides the dynamic for Deleuze's exposition of Bergson's position; it is as if Deleuze has merely descended one level deeper into Hegel's logic of being, with Bergson, his Virgil, close at his side.

It should come as no surprise, therefore, that when Deleuze approaches the problem of the One and the Multiple in *Bergsonism*, his critique of the dialectical solution is very similar to the earlier critique of the dialectical process of determination. "There are many theories in philosophy that combine the one and the multiple. They share the characteristic of claiming to reconstruct the real with general ideas" (*Bergsonism* 43-44). Deleuze provides us with two examples of this generalizing negative movement: "We are told that the Self is one (thesis) and it is multiple (antithesis), then it is the unity of the multiple (synthesis). Or else we are told that the One is already multiple, that Being passes into nonbeing and produces becoming" (44). Deleuze has three arguments ready in his arsenal from the earlier attack on determination. (1) Contradiction is a misreading of difference that can only be achieved by posing general, imprecise terms that are abstract from reality. Being in general, nonbeing in general, the One in general, the Multiple in general: These terms are too large, too abstract to grasp the specificity and singularity of reality; they are cut too big and hang loosely on reality, as Bergson says, "like baggy clothes" (44). (2) The negative movement of the dialectic violates the real relations of being. "Bergson criticizes the dialectic for being a *false movement*, that is, a movement of the abstract concept, which goes from one opposite to the other only by means of imprecision" (44). As we found earlier, polemics about false and real movements of being have their foundation in causal ontological arguments: The dialectic of contradiction can only imply *causae per accidens*. (3) Finally, the dialectical synthesis cannot grasp the plane of reality by combining opposed abstract concepts:

> Of what use is a dialectic that believes itself to be reunited with the real when it compensates for the inadequacy of a concept that is too broad or too general by invoking the opposite concept, which is no less broad and general? The concrete will never be attained by combining the inadequacy of one concept with the inadequacy of its opposite. The singular will never be attained by correcting a generality with another generality. (44)

As we have noted, the principle that an effect cannot contain more reality than its cause denies the power of the dialectical synthesis to move from abstraction to reality, from generality to singularity.

We should pause for a moment, though, to evaluate Deleuze's characterization of the dialectic. "The Self is one (thesis) and it is multiple (antithesis), then it is the unity of the multiple (synthesis)"—certainly, Hegel's treatment of the One and the Multiple is much more complex than this. Is Deleuze merely setting up a straw man? A Hegelian could well object that Deleuze's characterization is presented in "inappropriate form" since it expresses the One and the Multiple as propositions: "This truth is to be grasped and expressed only as a becoming, as a process, a repulsion and attraction—not as being, which in a proposition has the character of a stable unity" (*Science of Logic* 172). This is certainly a valid charge against Deleuze's mock dialectic; we have seen elsewhere, however, that Deleuze's principal charge is not that the dialectic fails to recognize being in terms of a dynamic, a process, but that the movement of the dialectic is a false movement. Let us venture into the complexity of Hegel's argument, then, to gauge the validity of Deleuze's attack. For Hegel, the movement between the One and the Multiple represents a higher level of mediation than the movement of determination and constitutes a logical passage from the quality to the quantity of being. Determinate being, the result of the previous development, gives way to the abstract, posited unity of being-for-one. This One enters the quantitative domain through the dialectical process of repulsion and attraction, which is simultaneously internal and external in its complex movement of self-relation:

> The one as *infinitely self*-related—infinitely, as the posited negation of negation—is the mediation in which it repels from itself its own self as its absolute (that is, abstract) *otherness*, (the *many*), and in relating itself

negatively to this its non-being, that is, in sublating it, it is only self-
relation; and one is only this *becoming* in which it is no longer
determined as having a *beginning*, that is, is no longer posited as an
immediate, affirmative being, neither is it as result, as having restored
itself as the one, that is, the one as equally *immediate* and excluding; the
process which it is posits and contains it throughout only as sublated.
(*Science of Logic* 177)

The infinitely self-related one, a posited indetermination, enters into relation with its abstract and multiple other, its nonbeing, and through the
sublation of this opposition we get the becoming of the One, a realized
ideality.

It is very easy to apply Deleuze's charges against the negative ontological movement to this passage. The initial movement of the One into its opposite, into its nonbeing, is completely external and can only imply an accidental relation. Furthermore, this movement between terms (Hegel calls
them "absolute") claims to arrive at a determinate synthesis. "The one one
. . . is the realized ideality, posited in the one; it is attraction through the
mediation of repulsion, and it contains this mediation with itself as *its determination*" (174). The mere fact of abstract mediation results in a real
determination. As we have seen, just as Deleuze charges that external mediation implies an accidental relation, he also refuses a dialectics of contradictions the power of real synthesis: The "combining" and "joining" of
abstract terms cannot have a real, concrete result. To these two attacks we
can add the charge that the very terms that Hegel uses are imprecise. For
this argument, Deleuze invokes Plato and his metaphor of the good cook
who takes care to make his cuts in the right place according to the articulations of reality (see *Bergsonism* 45 and "Bergson" 295). What Hegelian
terminology lacks is close attention to the specificity and singularity of real
being: Hegel appears as a careless dialectical butcher when compared to
Plato's fine talents. To arrive at a singular conception of unity and multiplicity in real being we have to begin by asking, in Platonic fashion, Which
being, which unity, which plurality? "What Bergson calls for—against the
dialectic, against a general conception of opposites (the One and the
Multiple)—is an acute perception of the 'what' and the 'how many' of what
he calls the 'nuance' or the potential number" (*Bergsonism* 45).

What has Deleuze gained, then, in this second phase of Bergson study,
by refocusing his attack from the problem of determination to that of the
One and the Multiple, from the discussion of quality to the passage from
quality to quantity? As always, Hegel is very clear about the stakes in the
discussion. Describing the defects of the conception of one and many
among the ancient atomists, who give precedence to multiplicity, he pro-

vides a suggestive analogy: "Physics with its molecules and particles suffers from the atom, this principle of extreme externality, which is thus utterly devoid of the Notion, just as much as does the theory of the State which starts from the particular will of individuals" (*Science of Logic* 167). The passage from quality to quantity reveals at the heart of an ontological problem, a political problem. The stakes are quite high. It is clear to Hegel that the relationship between the One and the Multiple is an (analogical) foundation for a theory of social organization, an ontological basis for politics. To attack the dialectical unity of the One and the Multiple, then, is to attack the primacy of the State in the formation of society, to insist on the real plurality of society. Here we begin to see traces of the movement that has taken place in Deleuze's "eight-year hole": The slight shift in focus in his attack on Hegelian logic, from chapter 2 to chapter 3 of "The Doctrine of Being," brings ontology into the sphere of politics.

What this new attack gives rise to specifically is a new conception of multiplicity. "The notion of multiplicity saves us from thinking in terms of 'One and Multiple' " (*Bergsonism* 43). This is where Deleuze manages to establish his preferred triangular configuration of enemies, because we find there are two types of multiplicities. The proximate enemies are G. B. R. Riemann and Albert Einstein; these thinkers are able to conceive of multiplicities, but merely of numerical, quantitative multiplicities that only succeed in grasping differences of degree (32-34). Bergson, in contrast, realizes a qualitative multiplicity founded on differences of nature. The first, the multiplicity of exteriority, is a multiplicity of "order"; Bergson's internal multiplicity is a multiplicity of "organization" (*Bergsonism* 38). The Hegelian dialectic, of course, occupies the third, extreme position, unable to think multiplicity at all because it recognizes neither differences of nature nor differences of degree. The configuration of proximate enemies, though, allows Deleuze's Bergson a detachment from the Hegelian terrain: "For Bergson it is not a question of opposing the Multiple to the One but, on the contrary, of distinguishing two types of multiplicity" (39). We will return to analyze this positive project of multiplicity below, but it is important now to recognize the clarity of the political framework of the project that has resulted from the critique: Deleuze has created a position to advocate a pluralism of organization against a pluralism of order. And this is far removed from Hegel's State philosophy of the unity of the One and the Multiple.

1.3 The Positive Emanation of Being

Let us turn now from the aggressive moment directed against the Hegelian dialectic to the positive alternative that Deleuze finds in Bergson. The

terms of the alternative are already given by the critique: Through a positive, internal movement, being must become qualified and concrete in its
singularity and specificity. This issue of quality is common in both of
Deleuze's periods of Bergson study, but since, as we noted, Deleuze's concerns move to the passage from quality to quantity in the second period,
Bergson's alternative logic of being must also address the question of unity
and multiplicity. We can begin to approach Bergson's position by trying to
situate it in traditional ontological terms. In effect, we do find a conception
of pure being in Bergson: The virtual is the simplicity of being, in itself,
pure recollection (*le souvenir pur*). However, pure, virtual being is not abstract and indifferent, and neither does it enter into relation with what is
other than itself—it is real and qualified through the internal process of
differentiation: "Difference is not a determination but, in this essential relationship with life, a differentiation" ("La conception de la différence chez
Bergson" 93). Being differs with itself immediately, internally. It does not
look outside itself for an other or a force of mediation because its difference rises from its very core, from "the explosive internal force that life
carries within itself" ("La conception de la différence chez Bergson" 93).[8]
This *élan vital* that animates being, this vital process of differentiation,
links the pure essence and the real existence of being: "Virtuality exists in
such a way that it is realized in dissociating itself, that it is forced to disso-
ciate itself in order to realize itself. Differention is the movement of a virtuality that is actualizng itself" (93). Bergson sets up, then, two concepts of
being: Virtual being is pure, transcendental being in that it is infinite and
simple; actualized being is real being in that it is different, qualified, and
limited. We have already seen how Deleuze focuses on ontological movement as the locus of Bergson's originality. The central constructive task of
Deleuze's reading of Bergson, then, is to elaborate the positive movement
of being between the virtual and the actual that supports the necessity of
being and affords being both sameness and difference, both unity and
multiplicity.

    This discussion of ontological movement relies on Bergson's claim of a
fundamental difference between time and space, between duration and
matter.[9] Space is only capable of containing differences of degree and thus
presents merely a quantitative variation; time contains differences of nature and thus is the true medium of substance. "The division occurs between duration, which 'tends' for its part to take on or bear all the differences of nature (because it is endowed with the power of qualitatively
varying with itself), and space, which never presents anything but differences of degree (since it is a quantitative homogeneity)" (*Bergsonism* 31,
modified). Duration is the domain in which we can find the primary ontological movement because duration, which is composed of differences

of nature, is able to differ qualitatively with itself. Space, or matter, which contains only differences of degree, is the domain of modal movement because space cannot differ with itself, but rather repeats. "Everything that Bergson says always comes back to this: duration is *what differs with itself*. Matter, on the contrary, is what does not differ with itself, what repeats" ("La conception de la différence chez Bergson" 88). The ontological criterion assumed here is differing with self, internal difference. Once again, the discussion appears as a simple transposition of causal foundations of being: Substance that is cause of itself (*causa sui*) becomes substance that differs with itself. Indeed, Deleuze characterizes the distinction between duration and matter precisely in the traditional terms of a substance-mode relationship: "Duration is like a *natura naturans*, and matter a *natura naturata*" (*Bergsonism* 93, modified). Why is it, though, that duration can differ with itself and matter cannot? The explanation follows from our first observations about Bergson's difference. The discussion of difference in Bergson is not directed toward distinguishing a quidditas or a state; it is not oriented toward a *location* of essence, but rather toward the identification of an essential movement, a process, in time. In the second phase of Bergson study, Deleuze extends this distinction between duration and matter to the two distinct types of multiplicity: Space reveals a multiplicity of exteriority, a numerical multiplicity of quantitative differentiation, a multiplicity of order; pure duration presents an internal multiplicity, a heterogeneity of qualitative differentiation, a multiplicity of organization (*Bergsonism* 38). Furthermore, Deleuze argues not only that the domain of duration provides a more profound multiplicity than space, but also that it poses a more profound unity. The modal nature of space, in effect, does not afford it an inherent unity. To recognize the essential nature of being as a substantial unity, then, we have to think being in terms of time: "a single Time, one, universal, impersonal" (78).

Now that along with Bergson and Deleuze we have adopted an ontological perspective firmly grounded in duration, we still need to see how the virtual and the actual communicate. Bergson's discussion is very strong in analyzing the unfolding of the virtual in the actual—what Deleuze calls the process of differentiation or actualization. In this regard, Bergson is a philosopher of the emanation of being, and the Platonic resonances are very strong. This is precisely the context in which Deleuze notes the Platonic passage very dear to Bergson in which he compares the philosopher to the good cook, "who cuts according to the natural articulations" ("Bergson" 295). Recognizing the contour of being in the real differences of nature is the task of the philosopher, because the process of differentiation is the basic movement of life. *Elan vital* is presented in exactly these terms: "It is always a case of a virtuality in the process of being actualized, a simplicity in the process of differentiating, a totality in the process of dividing: Proceeding 'by dissociation and division,' by 'dichotomy,' is the essence of life" (*Bergsonism* 94). Pure being—as virtuality, simplicity, totality— emanates or actualizes through a process of differentiation, a process that marks or cuts along the lines of the differences of nature. This is how differentiation addresses the ontological criteria of quality and quantity: Virtual being, as unity, unfolds and reveals its real multiple differences. However, we should be careful not to exaggerate the similarities to Platonism. There are at least two aspects that distinguish Deleuze's description of Bergsonian actualization from Platonic emanation. First, Deleuze claims that the actualization of "the virtual Whole" is not a degradation of being—it is not the limitation or copying of the ideal in the real—but instead Bergson's actualization is the positive production of the actuality and multiplicity of the world: "One only has to replace the actual terms in the movement that produces them, that is bring them back to the virtuality actualized in them, in order to see that differentiation is never a negation but a creation, and that difference is never negative but essentially positive and creative" (*Bergsonism* 103). Second, as we have seen, Deleuze argues that Bergson's ontological movement relies on an absolutely immanent, efficient production of being driven by "the explosive internal force that life carries within itself." There is no room for Platonic finalism as a force of order. In this context, then, we can understand Bergson's ontological movement as creative emanation of being free from the order of the Platonic Ideal (105-6).

However, as Deleuze makes very clear, if we are to understand Bergson's emanation of being correctly, we should not conceive it as a differentiation in space but an "actualization" in time. (Note that here the discussion relies heavily on the primary French meaning of *actuel* as "contemporary.") This is where Bergson's theory of memory comes into play. In the past Bergson finds pure being—"a recollection that is pure, virtual, impassive, inactive, *in itself*" (*Bergsonism* 71). The creative movement from the past unity to the present multiplicity is the process of actualization. Situating Bergson's emanation of being in time allows Deleuze to demonstrate the force of his terminology, which reveals the important difference between Bergson's and other conceptions of ontological movement. This discussion is presented through an enigmatic constellation of terms that constitutes a very complex argument. The general goal of this discussion is to offer an adequate critique of the notion of the possible. Deleuze asserts that it is essential that we conceive of the Bergsonian emanation of being, differentiation, as a relationship between the *virtual* and the *actual*, rather than as a relationship between the *possible* and the *real*.[10] After setting up these two couples (virtual-actual and possible-real),

Deleuze proceeds to note that the transcendental term of each couple relates positively to the immanent term of the opposite couple. The possible
is never real, even though it may be actual; however, while the virtual may
not be actual, it is nonetheless real. In other words, there are several contemporary (actual) possibilities of which some may be realized in the future; in contrast, virtualities are always real (in the past, in memory) and
may become actualized in the present. Deleuze invokes Proust for a definition of the states of virtuality: "real without being actual, ideal without
being abstract" (96). The essential point here is that the virtual is real and
the possible is not: This is Deleuze's basis for asserting that the movement
of being must be understood in terms of the virtual-actual relationship
rather than the possible-real relationship. To understand this evaluation we
need once again to refer to the causal arguments of Scholastic ontology. A
fundamental principle of causality that we had occasion to invoke earlier is
that an effect cannot have more reality than its cause. The ontological
movement from the virtual to the actual is consistent with this principle
since the virtual is just as real as the actual. The progression from the possible to the real, however, is clearly a violation of this principle and on this
basis must be rejected as a model of ontological movement. We should
note that, even though Deleuze makes no explicit reference to the Scholastics here, the mode of explanation and the very terms of the discussion
are thoroughly Scholastic. Virtual is the Scholastic term to describe the
ideal or transcendental; the virtual Scholastic God is not in any way abstract
or possible, it is the *ens realissimum*, the most real being. Finally, actualization is the Scholastic means of describing the familiar Aristotelian passage from the virtual into act.[11] In this context, Bergson's usage becomes
even more interesting: Bergson's "actualization" maintains the Aristotelian
meaning and adds to it the temporal dimension suggested by the modern
French usage. In Bergson, the passage from virtuality to act takes place only
in duration.

What is at stake for Deleuze in this enigmatic group of terms — in rejecting the possible and advocating "actualization" over "realization" — is
the very nature of the emanation of being and the principle that directs
it. Deleuze elaborates this evaluation by adding a further constellation
of terms. The process of realization is guided by two rules: resemblance
and limitation. On the contrary, the process of actualization is guided by
difference and creation. Deleuze explains that, from the first point of
view, the real is thought to be in the image of (thus to *resemble*) the possible that it realizes — "it simply has existence or reality added to it, which
is translated by saying that, from the point of view of the concept, there is
no *difference* between the possible and the real" (*Bergsonism* 97, emphasis added). Furthermore, since all the possibilities cannot be realized,

since the realm of the possible is greater than the realm of the real, there must be a process of *limitation* that determines which possibilities will "pass" into reality. Thus, Deleuze finds a sort of preformism in the couple possibility-reality, in that all of reality is already given or determined in the possible; reality preexists itself in the "pseudo-actuality" of the possible and only emanates through a limitation guided by resemblances (98). Therefore, since there is no difference between the possible and the real (from the point of view of the concept), since the image of reality is already given in the possible, the passage of realization cannot be a creation.

On the contrary, in order for the virtual to become actual, it must *create* its own terms of actualization. "The reason for this is simple: While the real is the image and likeness of the possible that it realizes, the actual, on the other hand does *not* resemble the virtuality that it embodies" (*Bergsonism* 97). The *difference* between the virtual and the actual is what requires that the process of actualization be a *creation*. With no preformed order to dictate its form, the process of the actualization of being must be a creative evolution, an original production of the multiplicity of actual being through differentiation. We can partially understand this complex discussion as a critique of the movement of the formal cause (possible-real) and an affirmation of that of the efficient cause (virtual-actual). The stakes of the discussion appear more clearly, though, if we pose the issue in terms of the principle that determines the coherence of being, as a critique of *order* and an affirmation of *organization*. Earlier we cited a distinction that Deleuze makes between the "multiplicity of order" and the "multiplicity of organization" (38). The realization of the possible clearly gives rise to a multiplicity of order, a static multiplicity, because all of real being is pregiven or predetermined in the "pseudo-actuality" of the possible. The actualization of the virtual, on the other hand, presents a dynamic multiplicity in which the process of differentiation creates the original arrangement or coherence of actual being: This is the multiplicity of organization. The multiplicity of order is "determinate" in that it is preformed and static; the multiplicity of organization is "indeterminate" in that it is creative and original—organization is always unforeseeable.[12] Without the blueprint of order, the creative process of organization is always an art.

We have shown that Deleuze presents the Bergsonian actualization of being as a dynamic and original emanation, as a creative evolution free from the ordering restraints of both Platonic finalism (final cause) and the realization of the possible (formal cause). However, this formulation begs the important question, which has been inherent in the discussion all along: Free from any determined order or preformism, what constitutes the creative mechanism in Bergsonian being that is capable of continually forming a new, original being, a new plane of composition? What is the basis of Bergsonian organization? This is precisely the point on which one could mount a Hegelian counteroffensive. If we return to Hegel's critique of Spinoza we can recognize a pressure that also applies to Bergson's position. Hegel finally characterizes Spinoza's positive movement of being as an unrecuperative emanationism:

> In the oriental conception of *emanation* the absolute is the light which illumines itself. Only it not only illumines itself but also *emanates*. Its emanations are *distancings* from its undimmed clarity; the successive productions are less perfect than the preceding ones from which they arise. The process of emanation is taken only as a *happening*, the becoming only as a progressive loss. Thus being increasingly obscures itself and night, the negative, is the final term of the series, which does not return to the primal light. (*Science of Logic* 538-39)

Clearly, it is true that Bergson's movement, like that of Spinoza, does lack the "reflection-into-self" that Hegel identifies as the missing element here. However, as we have seen, Bergson insists that "successive productions" are not "less perfect"; the movement is not a "progressive loss," but rather, the differentiation constituted by *élan vital* is a creative process that produces new equally perfect articulations. Bergson might very well respond in Spinozian fashion that actuality is perfection. However, the Hegelian attack serves as a pressure to back up this Bergsonian claim with an immanent creative mechanism. Hegel recognizes that a positive ontological movement can account for the becoming of being (as emanation), but, he asks, How can it account for the being of becoming? Furthermore, Hegel's analogy between physics and politics returns as a serious political challenge. Along with the ancient atomists, Deleuze and Bergson refuse the preformism of the multiplicity in the unity; they refuse the order of the State, and insist instead on the originality and freedom of the multiplicity of organization. From a Hegelian perspective, this is just as mad as trying to base a State on the individual wills of its citizens. The attack on order (the order of finalism, of the possible, of the dialectic) creates both the space for and the need for an organizational dynamic: the organization of the actual, the organization of the multiplicity. Responding to this is the final task posed in Deleuze's reading of Bergson.

1.4 The Being of Becoming and the Oganization of the Actual

The question of creative organization poses a serious problem, and, finally, this is the point on which Bergson's thought seems to prove insufficient for Deleuze. The need for actual organization obviously becomes much more important as Deleuze moves to his second phase of Bergson study, as he shifts focus from the issue of quality to the passage between quality and quantity. In our analysis up to this point we have seen that Bergson is very effective in describing the emanative movement from a unity to a multiplicity, the process of differentiation or actualization. But now we discover a need for a complementary organizational movement in the opposite direction, from a multiplicity to a unity. Unfortunately, this organizational movement is nearly absent in Bergson's thought. There are, nonetheless, several points at which Deleuze's reading suggests that we might find an answer to this need in Bergson. Deleuze seems to suggest that there is a convergent movement of the actual: "The real is not only that which is cut out [*se découpe*] according to natural articulations or differences of nature; it is also that which intersects again [*se recoupe*] along paths converging toward the same ideal or virtual point" (*Bergsonism* 29). What exactly is this process of *recoupement* or intersection that relates the actual multiplicity to a virtual unity? Deleuze does not treat this point extensively. It seems, however, that in order to make sense of this passage we cannot read *recoupement* as a creative process that organizes a new virtual point of unity, but rather merely as a process that traces the lines of the natural articulations back to the original point of departure. *Recoupement* is a Bergsonian way of expressing the Scholastic principle that being is univocal; we can verify that being is always and everywhere said in the same way, that is, because all of reality can be traced back along convergent paths to one unique virtual point. This theory of univocity opposes a theory of the analogy of being. What is important for us here is that while univocity implies a general equality and commonality of being, it does so only on the virtual plane.[13] What we are in need of, however, is a means of communication between the two planes. This passage suggests, and indeed we often find in Bergson's work, that the unity only appears on the plane of the virtual. What Deleuze's argument demands at this point, on the contrary, is a mechanism for the organization of the actual multiplicity.

We find another example of the communication between the virtual and the actual in Bergson's two movements of memory: the "recollection-memory" that dilates or enlarges in an inclusive movement toward the past and the "contraction-memory" that concentrates toward the future as a process of particularization (*Bergsonism* 52). In other words, looking backward we see the universal (recollection-memory) and looking forward we see the individual (contraction-memory). What would be necessary for the creative organization of the actual, on the contrary, would be an enlarging, inclusive movement oriented toward the future capable of producing a new unity. However, Bergson is insistent on the temporal directions of the movements. The unity of the virtual resides only in the past and we can never really move backward toward that point: "We do not move from the present to the past, from perception to recollection, but from the past to the present, from recollection to perception" (63). In these terms, the organization of the actual would have to be a movement from perception to a new "recollection" that would be a future memory (a sort of *futur antérieur* or future perfect in the grammatical sense) as a common point of real organization.

Deleuze does his best to address seriously the question of organization and socialization in the final pages of *Bergsonism* (106-12). In many of his major works (in his studies of both Nietzsche and Spinoza, for example), Deleuze presents in the final pages his densest and most elusive argument that points the way toward future research. In this final section of *Bergsonism*, Deleuze tries to explain the human capacity for creativity, the capability to take control of the process of differentiation or actualization and to go beyond the "plane" or "plan" of nature: "Man is capable of burning the plans, of going beyond both his own plan and his own condition, in order finally to express naturing Nature [*natura naturans*]" (107). The explanation of this human freedom and creativity, though, is not immediately obvious. Certainly, society is formed on the basis of human intelligence, but Deleuze notes that there is not a direct movement between intelligence and society. Instead, society is more directly a result of "irrational factors." Deleuze identifies "virtual instinct" and "the fable-making function" (*la fonction fabulatrice*) as the forces that lead to the creation of obligations and of gods. These forces, however, cannot account for the human powers of creativity.[14]

For solution, we have to go back to analyze the gap that exists between human intelligence and socialization. "What is it that appears in the interval between intelligence and society . . . ? We cannot reply: It is intuition" (109). The intuition is that same "explosive internal force that life carries within itself" that we noted earlier as the positive dynamic of being. Here, however, this notion is filled out more clearly. More precisely, Deleuze adds soon after, what fills this gap between intelligence and sociability is the origin of intuition, which is creative emotion (110). This original production of sociability through creative emotion leads us back to Bergson's plane of unity in memory, but this time it is a new memory. "And what is this creative emotion, if not precisely a cosmic Memory, that actualizes all the levels at the same time, that liberates man from the plan or the level to which he belongs, in order to make him a creator, adequate to the whole movement of creation?" (111, modified). With the cosmic Memory, Deleuze has arrived at a mystical Bergsonian sociability that is available to the "privileged souls" (111) and that is capable of tracing the design of an open society, a society of creators. The incarnation of the cosmic Memory "leaps from one soul to another, 'every now and then,' crossing closed deserts" (111). What we have here sounds distinctly like a weak echo of the voice of Zarathustra on the mountaintops: creative pathos, productive emotion, a community of active creators who go beyond the plane of nature and human beings. However, suggestive as this brief explanation of a Bergsonian social theory might be, it remains in this final section obscure and undeveloped. Furthermore, the rest of Deleuze's work on Bergson does not serve to support this theory. In effect, we have to refer to Deleuze's Nietzsche to give these claims real coherence and a solid grounding.[15]

This final section of *Bergsonism* is the most notable positive argument in the second phase of Bergson study that does not appear in the first, and it perfectly corresponds to the shift from the problematic of quality to that of the passage from quality to quantity that we noted in the attack on Hegel. This twofold shift between the two Bergson studies shows clearly one aspect of the movement that takes place in Deleuze's "eight-year hole"; in effect, Deleuze feels the pressure to bring the ontological to the social and the ethical. In *Bergsonism* Deleuze succeeds in addressing this pressure to an extent. More important, however, this reorientation announces the need for and the advent of Nietzsche in Deleuze's thought. Nietzsche gives Deleuze the means to explore the real being of becoming and the positive organization of the actual multiplicity. Furthermore, by shifting the terrain from the plane of logic to that of values, Nietzsche allows Deleuze to translate the positive ontology he has developed through the study of Bergson toward a positive ethics.

Remark: Deleuze and Interpretation

Before turning to Nietzsche, let us take a moment to consider two critiques of Deleuze's reading of Bergson that will help us clarify the characteristics of Deleuze's interpretative strategy. At the outset of our essay, we noted that the peculiarities of Deleuze's work require that we keep a series of methodological principles in mind. One aspect that makes Deleuze's work so unusual is that he brings to each of his philosophical studies a very specific question that focuses and defines his vision. In the case of the Bergson studies, we have found that Deleuze is principally concerned with developing an adequate critique of the negative ontological movement of the dialectic and elaborating an alternative logic of the positive, creative movement of being. The selection involved in Deleuze's narrow focus is what seems to confuse some of his readers and to irritate others. The critiques of Gillian Rose ("The New Bergsonism") and Madeleine Barthélemy-Madaule ("Lire Bergson") offer us two examples of this problem. In these

critiques we can discern two methods of reading Deleuze that lead to interpretative difficulties: First, by failing to recognize Deleuze's selectivity,
these authors conflate Deleuze's positions with those of the philosophers
he addresses, and second, by ignoring the evolution of Deleuze's thought,
they confuse the different projects that guide his various works. In addition, the diversity of perspective between these two critics will serve to il-
lustrate the slippage that results from the gap between the Anglophone and
the French traditions of Bergson interpretation.

Throughout "The New Bergsonism" (chapter 6 of *Dialectic of Nihilism*),
Rose reads Bergson's work and Deleuze's interpretation as if they constituted a perfect continuum. She concludes her brief discussion of *Bergsonism* with an ambiguous attribution that illustrates this confusion very
clearly: "On Deleuze's reading Bergson produces a *Naturphilosophie*
which culminates at the point when *élan vital* 'becomes conscious of itself'
in the memory of 'man' " (Rose 101). To back this claim she cites the final
page of *Bergsonism* (112 in the English edition), which supports the second half of her sentence in part but does not support the first half at all.
Not only does Deleuze not mention *Naturphilosophie* in this passage, but
he has spent the previous pages (106-12) arguing that Bergson shows how
we can go beyond the plan of nature and create a new human nature, beyond the human condition. Here Deleuze is drawing principally on Bergson's late work *Les deux sources de la morale et de la religion* (1932). Rose
derives the idea of *Naturphilosophie* not from Deleuze but from Bergson's
earliest work, *Essai sur les données immédiates de la conscience* (1889),
which she reads as consistent with the work of Comte (Rose 98). (Therefore, to add to the confusion, we have a completely ahistorical reading of
Bergson that fails to distinguish between his early and late works.) The
central point here, though, is not that Bergson's thought does or does not
constitute a *Naturphilosophie*; rather, it is that this aspect does not form a
part of Deleuze's project, that this is not what Deleuze takes from Bergson.

We find a similar problem of interpretation in the essay by Madeleine
Barthélemy-Madaule, a French Bergson specialist, and it is interesting that
in her reading it is precisely these same pages of *Bergsonism* that create
the greatest irritation. Her reaction, however, comes from a very different
perspective from that of Rose, since she is grounded in the French spiritual
reading of Bergson rather than the Anglo-Saxon positivist reading.
Barthélemy-Madaule's primary objection is that Deleuze tries to read *Les
deux sources* as a Nietzschean and antihumanist text when in fact it demonstrates the profoundly religious character of Bergson's thought: "The
process of 'going beyond the human condition,' which is in effect the vo-
cation of philosophy for Bergson, cannot be formulated in terms of the
'inhuman' or the 'superhuman.' . . . In any case, the principal conclusion

that we take from this interpretation is that Bergson is not Nietzsche" ("Lire Bergson" 86, 120). Barthélemy-Madaule is a very careful reader of Bergson and, to a certain extent, one has to accept her criticism. Bergson is indeed not Nietzsche. For our purposes, Deleuze's (perhaps strained and unsuccessful) effort to bring the two together in these pages indicates the important effect that the period of Nietzsche study has had on his thought and the need to move beyond the Bergsonian framework. The main issue at stake in the conflict with Barthélemy-Madaule, however, is how one interprets a philosopher. Barthélemy-Madaule is reacting primarily against Deleuze's principle of selection: "Interpreting a doctrine supposes that one has accounted for all the terms of the ensemble. Now it does not seem to me that this is the case here. I would contest Mr. Deleuze's use of *Bergsonism* as the title of his study" (120). The first type of problem in reading Deleuze, then, which we find in both Rose and Barthélemy-Madaule, results from a failure to recognize or accept Deleuze's selectivity and, thus, from a confusion both of his use of sources and of his relationship to the philosopher he studies.

The second type of problem results from a misreading of Deleuze's projects, from a failure to recognize Deleuze's evolution. This problem arises primarily in Rose's critique. It is certainly strange that when Rose seeks to engage Deleuze's work in relation to her general theme about juridicism and poststructuralism she would choose to read *Bergsonism*— any of his other studies in the history of philosophy (on Kant, Hume, Nietzsche, or Spinoza) would have been more adequate to her task. As we have seen, Deleuze's investigation of Bergson is focused primarily on ontological issues, and, although it flirts with the question of ethics, it gives no solid grounds for a discussion of law. With this in mind, then, it should come as no surprise that Rose has difficulty writing directly about Deleuze's Bergson. In fact, she dedicates less than two of the twenty-one pages to *Bergsonism* (99-100); these are prefaced by a reading of Bergson's *Essai sur les données immédiates de la conscience* in relation to Comte and positivism and followed by a reading of sections of Deleuze's *Différence et répétition*, combined with small additions from Nietzsche and Duns Scotus. Rose repeatedly refers to the intent of Deleuze's new Bergsonism as the attempt to found an "ontological injustice" (99, 104, 108). She substantiates this claim with a quote from a section of *Différence et répétition* in which Deleuze is discussing the univocity of being in Duns Scotus, Nietzsche, and Spinoza: "Univocal Being is both nomadic distribution and crowned anarchy" (quoted by Rose 99, Deleuze 55). The problem here is quite simple: In the cited passage, Deleuze is dealing neither with Bergson nor with justice. I have argued that in Deleuze's treatment of Bergson we can find the suggestion of a concept of univocal being, but that does not mean that we can transfer the Duns Scotus-Spinoza-Nietzsche nexus directly to Bergson: This is a simple methodological issue. More important, though, this passage reveals the inadequacy of Rose's entire argument. It is absurd to read the statement that univocal being is "crowned anarchy" as a directly political statement, or even as a statement about justice. Such a claim attempts to collapse a complex development from ontology to politics and to assume that such a development admits only one solution. (This is apparently how Rose can come to the point of attributing Scotus's ethics to Deleuze [107]—with the belief, one must assume, that there can only be one ethics that corresponds to a univocal conception of being.) At the very most, univocity gives us an intuition of politics through its implication of an ontological equality and participation; this equality is what "crowns" the anarchy of being in Deleuze's account (*Différence et répétition* 55). I would maintain, however, that in order to bring this intuition to a veritable conception of justice in Deleuze's thought, to move in effect from ontology to politics, we need to pass through at least two more important phases. First, we must look at the conception of efficient power (force internal to its manifestation) developed in the study of Nietzsche, because this founds an attack on law and juridicism.[16] Second, we must turn to the study of Spinoza for its investigation of common notions, of socially constitutive practice and of right, so that Deleuze can elaborate a positive alternative to law. *Jus* versus *lex*: This a much more adequate formulation of Deleuze's position against legalism and juridicism.

Chapter 2

Nietzschean Ethics
From Efficient Power to an Ethics of Affirmation

In order to appreciate Deleuze's work on Nietzsche we have to situate it in the context of the development of Deleuze's own project. *Nietzsche and Philosophy* is the concrete result of the "eight-year hole" in Deleuze's intellectual life, the longest gap in his prolific career. According to Deleuze, though, such a gap is not indicative of inactivity; on the contrary, "perhaps it is in the holes that the movement takes place" ("Signes et événements" 18). The work on Nietzsche, then, will perhaps give us a key to reading the movement that animates Deleuze's early work. This study of Nietzsche is the intervention that gives rise to the important differences between the two phases of Bergson study that we discussed in chapter 1. We can summarize this reorientation by saying that Bergson's positive, logical dynamism has entered a new horizon, a field of forces, where all the logical issues are posed now in terms of sense and value. On this new terrain, all kinds of new figures immediately spring up. Most important, the heart of the Bergsonian logical discussion is transformed into an analysis of the nature of power. The analysis of power provides the basis for the fundamental passage in Deleuze's study of Nietzsche: from the ontological foundation of power to the ethical creation of being. Finally, we should refer the study of Nietzsche not only back to the previous work on Bergson, but also forward to the subsequent study of Spinoza. We will find that Deleuze's construction of an ethical horizon within the framework of Nietzsche's thought brings to light the questions that make possible (or indeed necessary) his subsequent investigation of Spinozian practice.

2.1 The Paradox of Enemies

In the study of Nietzsche, as in that of Bergson, Deleuze's analysis is driven by an antagonism toward Hegel. Here, however, Deleuze's strategy of triangulation that we discussed earlier (Section 1.1) becomes more complicated and more ambiguous. Although *Nietzsche and Philosophy* contains some of Deleuze's harshest rhetoric against Hegel, the polemical focus is already moving away from Hegel in important ways. As in the Bergson studies, Deleuze brings in other antagonists who are closer to Nietzsche's position and who share some of his concerns in order to maintain the vast distance from Hegel; Deleuze refuses to descend and struggle on Hegel's own terrain. Once again, we find that Hegel inherits the faults of the proximate antagonists and takes them to their extreme, as a sort of negative raising to the nth power.

The ambiguities in Deleuze's position, however, are all those related to his developing conceptions of antagonism and opposition. Deleuze gives seemingly contradictory indications about the best way to choose and relate to one's enemy. In several passages, we find that Deleuze views the fundamental antagonism toward Hegel as an urgent and central element of his reading of Nietzsche: "We will misunderstand the whole of Nietzsche's work if we do not see 'against whom' its principal concepts are directed. Hegelian themes are present in this work as the enemy against which it fights" (162). "Anti-Hegelianism runs through Nietzsche's work as its cutting edge" (8). And finally, Nietzsche's philosophy forms "an absolute anti-dialectics" (195). In these passages the need for a direct confrontation with Hegel is very clear. In other passages, however, Deleuze tries to displace the relationship to Hegel, to destroy its binary character with the same type of triangular configuration we found in the Bergson studies:

> Nietzsche's relation to Kant is like Marx's to Hegel: Nietzsche stands
> critique on its feet, just as Marx does with the dialectic. . . . the dialectic
> comes from the original Kantian form of the critique. There would have
> been no need to put the dialectic back on its feet, nor "to do" any form
> of dialectics if critique itself had not been standing on its head from the
> start. (89)

In this passage it seems that Hegel is not of real concern to Nietzsche; the dialectic constitutes a false problem. Instead, Nietzsche addresses Kant as his proximate enemy. These two stances form a paradox: Is Nietzsche's primary antagonism with Kant, the proximate enemy, or with Hegel, the ultimate enemy? Deleuze has to navigate between Scylla and Charybdis. Posing Nietzsche as the ultimate anti-Hegel presents a real danger; Nietzsche appears in the position of negation, of reaction, of *ressentiment*. And furthermore, absolute opposition seems (in a Hegelian framework) to imply the initiation of a new dialectical process. However, if we try instead to focus only on a proximate enemy (such as Kant) and do not recognize anti-Hegelianism as the fundamental driving force, "we will misunderstand the whole of Nietzsche's work" (162).

We can get a preliminary idea of Deleuze's treatment of this problem of enemies by looking at his reading of *The Birth of Tragedy*. Deleuze finds that this early text presents a "semi-dialectical" argument based on the Dionysus/Apollo antithesis (13). Deleuze gives an elegant explanation of this problem in terms of an evolution of Nietzsche's thought that resolves the antinomic couple in two directions: on one hand, toward a more profound opposition (Dionysus/Socrates or, later, Dionysus/Christ) and, on the other hand, toward a complementarity (Dionysus/Ariadne) (14). In the second couple, that of complementarity, the enemy has completely disappeared and the relationship is one of mutual affirmation; this couple is productive, but cannot suffice on its own because it does not provide Nietzsche a weapon with which to attack his enemies. The first couple does constitute a weapon, but in a problematical fashion. According to Deleuze, Nietzsche first shifts from Apollo to Socrates as the real enemy of Dionysus, but this proves insufficient because "Socrates is too Greek, a little too Apollonian at the outset because of his clarity, a little too Dionysian in the end" (14). When Socrates proves to be merely a proximate enemy, Nietzsche discovers the fundamental enemy in Christ. Here, however, with the Antichrist and the opposition and negation it implies, we seem to run the risk of initiating a new dialectic. Deleuze claims that this is not the case: "The opposition of Dionysus or Zarathustra to Christ is not a dialectical opposition, but opposition to the dialectic itself" (17). What exactly is this nondialectical negation, and what marks its difference from dialectical negation? We do not have the means to give the answer yet, but the question itself sets the tone and the task for Deleuze's reading. The answer will have to be found in Nietzsche's total critique; it must constitute an absolutely destructive negation that spares nothing from its force and recuperates nothing from its enemy; it must be an absolute aggression that offers no pardons, takes no prisoners, pillages no goods; it must mark the death of the enemy, with no resurrection. This is the radical, nondialectical negation that Deleuze's reading of Nietzsche must develop.

2.2 The Transcendental Method and the Partial Critique

Kant's enormous contribution to philosophy is to conceive of an immanent critique that is both total and positive. Kant, however, fails to carry out this project, and thus Nietzsche's role, according to Deleuze, is to correct Kant's errors and salvage the project (89). The principal fault of the Kantian critique is that of transcendental philosophy itself. In other words, Kant's discovery of a domain beyond the sensible is the creation of a region outside the bounds of the critique that effectively functions as a refuge against critical forces, as a limitation on critical powers. A total critique, on the contrary, requires a materialistic, monistic perspective in which the entire unified horizon is open and vulnerable to the critique's destabilizing inquiry. Therefore, it is the transcendental method itself that requires (or allows) that the critique remain partial. With the ideal values safely protected in the suprasensible, the Kantian critique can proceed to treat claims to truth and morality without endangering truth and morality themselves. Kant effectively grants immunity to the established values of the ruling order and "thus total critique turns into a politics of compromise" (89). Kant's critical reason functions to reinforce the established values and make us obedient to them: "When we stop obeying God, the State, our parents, reason appears and persuades us to continue being docile" (92). The very positing of the transcendental plane and the consequent partiality of the critique, then, is what allows Kantianism to be conservative. Under the cloak of disinterest, Kant appears as a passive State functionary, a traditional intellectual in Gramscian terms, legitimating the values of the ruling powers and protecting them from critical forces. Finally, Kant's critique is too polite, restrained by the "humble recognition of the rights of the criticised" (89). Kant is too genteel, too well mannered, too timid to question seriously the fundamental established values. In contrast, the total critique recognizes no restraints, no limits on its power, and is therefore necessarily insurrectional; a total critique must be an all-out attack on the established values and the ruling powers they support. Critique is always violence—this is not the real issue. The issue is the extent of, and the limits on, the reign of critique's destructive force.

The Kantian critique not only fails to be total, but it also fails to be positive; in effect, the failure to be total obstructs the possibility of being positive. The negative, destructive moment of the critique (*pars destruens*) that draws the total horizon into question and destabilizes previously existing powers must clear the terrain to allow the productive moment (*pars construens*) to release or create new powers—destruction opens the way for creation. Therefore, Kant's double failure is really one. This conclusion follows directly from Nietzsche's focus on values: "One of the principal motifs of Nietzsche's work is that Kant had not carried out a true critique because he was not able to pose the problem of critique in terms of values" (1). The partiality of the first destructive moment of the critique allows the essential established values to endure and therefore fails to clear the ground necessary for the value-creating, constructive power. The "active instance" (89) that the Kantian critique lacks is precisely that which truly legislates: To legislate is not to legitimate order and preserve values, but precisely the opposite, to create new values (91). This critique of values forces us to consider the question of interest and perspective. Since we can accept no transcendental standpoint external to the plane of forces that determines and legitimates absolute knowledge and universal values, we must locate the perspective on the immanent plane and identify the interests it serves. Therefore, the only possible principle of a total critique is perspectivism (90).

This attack on Kant's transcendental method, invoking perspectivism, goes hand in hand with the Nietzschean attack on Platonic idealism. Deleuze approaches this issue by considering "the form of the question" that animates philosophical inquiry. The central question for Platonic inquiry, Deleuze claims, is "Qu'est-ce que?": "What is beauty, what is justice, etc?" (76). Nietzsche, though, wants to change the central question to "Qui?": "Who is beautiful?," or rather, "Which one is beautiful?" Once again, the focus of the attack is the transcendental method. "Qu'est-ce que?" is the transcendental question par excellence that seeks an ideal that stands above, as a suprasensible principle ordering the various material instantiations. "Qui?" is a materialist question that looks to the movement of real forces from a specific perspective. In effect, the two questions point to different worlds for their answers. Deleuze will later call the materialist question "the method of dramatization" and insist that it is the primary form of inquiry throughout the history of philosophy (except perhaps in the work of Hegel).[1] The method of dramatization, then, is an elaboration of perspectivism as part of a critique of interest and value: "It is not enough to pose the abstract question 'what is truth?' (*qu'est-ce que le vrai*)"; rather we must ask "who wants truth (*qui veut le vrai*), when and where, how and how much?" ("La méthode de dramatisation" 95). The object of the attack in the question "Qu'est-ce que?" is the transcendental space that it implies, and that provides a sanctuary for established values from the destructive power of inquiry and critique. This transcendental space immune from the critique is the locus of order. We can certainly detect a Bergsonian inspiration in this argument. The question "Qu'est-ce que?" remains abstract because it implies two errors: (1) It seeks essence in a static quidditas rather than in a dynamic of movement (and thus can only reveal differences of degree, not differences of nature); and (2) it assumes either a formal or a final cause (the form of justice and truth, of the Just and the True) as the ordering principle of reality. The question "Qui?" that brings us to the terrain of will and value asks for an immanent dynamic of being, an internal, efficient force of differentiation.

Remark: Deleuze's Selection of the "Impersonal" Nietzsche

We must be careful with the question "Qui?", however, because in Deleuze's Nietzsche the answer it seeks will never be found in an individual or collective subject, but rather in a presubjective force or will. The difficulties presented for the English translation of this passage serve to highlight the problem: Hugh Tomlinson notes that "who" cannot function as a translation of "qui" because it directs inquiry toward a person; therefore, at Deleuze's suggestion he translates "qui" as "which one" (207, note 3). Deleuze tries to explain this nuance further in his preface to the English translation: "Here we must rid ourselves of all 'personalist' references. The one that . . . does not refer to an individual, to a person, but rather to an event, that is, to the forces in their various relationships in a proposition or a phenomenon, and the genetic relationship that determines these forces (power)" (xi). This insistence on the impersonal nature of the question "Qui?" casts a different light on Deleuze's charge that the question "Qu'est-ce que?" is abstract. The impersonal "Qui?" is not more concrete because it locates specific subjects or agents, but because it operates on the materialist terrain of an efficient causality.

It is often a strain to read Nietzsche without adopting personalist references. Not only is there a long tradition of reading Nietzsche in this way, but also it would not be difficult to cite several passages in which we cannot help but read Nietzsche "personally." Here we have a very clear example of Deleuze's selectivity. In effect, Deleuze brings a Bergsonian approach to Nietzsche so as to read him in logical terms, that is, as a logic of the will and value that animates the field of presubjective forces. Whenever we ask the question "Qui?" we are going to look to a certain will to power for the response (cf. 53). Deleuze's research moves from a Bergsonian logic of being to a Nietzschean logic of the will. It is clear, then, how Deleuze's selection fits in with the scope of his project. The "impersonal" interpretative strategy can also be seen as a political selection. In fact, Deleuze's reading has made such a profound impression on Nietzsche studies partly because it succeeds in making so much of Nietzsche's thought while avoiding or effectively diffusing the force of arguments about Nietzsche's individualism and reactionary politics, nearly all of which are centered around a "personalist" interpretation and selection. I will argue, however, that although this selection may be necessary for Deleuze, it is effectively this "impersonal" aspect that marks the limit of Deleuze's development of ethical and political veins in Nietzsche.

2.3 Slave Logic and Efficient Power

Thus far we have considered Deleuze's Nietzschean attacks on the proximate enemies, Kant and Plato. The direct Nietzschean attack on Hegel, the
fundamental enemy, appears first in Bergsonian form. As in the works on
Bergson, Deleuze's initial charge against the dialectic is once again that it is
driven by a negative movement that cannot arrive at a concrete, singular
conception of being. Contradiction and opposition can only give abstract
results (157) and can only lead to an abstract determination of being, blind
to its subtle nuances, to its singularity: "The being of Hegelian logic is
merely 'thought' being, pure and empty, that affirms itself by passing into
its own opposite. But this being was never different from its opposite, it
never had to pass into what it already was. Hegelian being is pure and
simple nothingness" (183). The core of this attack is that Hegelian being is
abstract, not really different from its opposite. Deleuze, however, provides
no substantial foundation for these claims here, and therefore they can
sound rather hollow unless we read Bergson's critique of determination
into them. We have seen that Bergson argues that difference is only conceived as opposition through an abstraction from real differences, by an
imprecise view of reality; real difference does not go "all the way" to opposition. Moreover, the movement implied by this Hegelian being "passing into its opposite" is a completely external, and thus false, movement
that can never move closer to a real, concrete affirmation. Hence, Hegelian
ontological movement remains abstract and accidental. In effect, Deleuze's
Nietzsche takes this Bergsonian analysis of the abstract character of the
negative ontological movement of determination for granted.

Once we recognize that Bergsonian arguments are functioning as the
foundation for this discussion, then, it should be no surprise that Deleuze
finds a Bergsonian alternative in Nietzsche: "For the speculative element of
negation, opposition or contradiction, Nietzsche substitutes the practical
element of *difference*" (9). This is very reminiscent of Bergson, except that
we can note that the terms of the conflict have become more concrete —
now the "speculative element" is contrasted with the "practical element."
In fact, the advent of Nietzsche in Deleuze's thought transforms the Bergsonian theoretical scene with a very important contribution. We no longer
have purely logical categories (external vs. internal difference, and negative vs. positive ontological movement), but now the logic is presented in
terms of volition and value (negation vs. affirmation, and interiority vs. exteriority). This shift to the horizon of forces marks the tendency in
Deleuze's thought that we noted earlier in the second phase of Bergson
study. The transposition to the terrain of values marks the beginning of our
trajectory from ontology to ethics and politics.

The complexity of this new terrain and the importance of Nietzsche's transformation become evident as Deleuze treats Nietzsche's polemic against slave logic and thereby develops a new attack on the Hegelian dialectic: "Nietzsche presents the dialectic as the speculation of the pleb, as the way of thinking of the slave: the abstract thought of contradiction then prevails over the concrete feeling of positive difference" (10). On this new terrain we have dramatic personae representing the two philosophical methods: the slave of abstract speculation versus the master of concrete pathos and practice. We are entering a very difficult passage, though, and should be careful to recognize from the outset the specific focus and polemical content of Deleuze's argument. Clearly, Deleuze is reading *On the Genealogy of Morals* as a harsh attack against Hegel—but against which Hegel? Since we are dealing with the master and the slave, it seems obvious that Deleuze's target is the *Phenomenology of Spirit*, or perhaps Kojève's popularized version of it. However, if we posit this as the focus, Deleuze's attack seems somewhat misdirected. In a very careful and intelligent study of *Nietzsche and Philosophy*, Jean Wahl notes the shortcomings of this attack: "Isn't there in the *Phenomenology of Spirit* something more profound that is able to resist the Nietzschean critique?" (364). Wahl is undoubtedly correct in noting that Deleuze's Nietzsche does not directly confront Hegel's central focus in the *Phenomenology*; but this should indicate to us that perhaps we have misinterpreted the primary target. Here we need to refine the first methodological principle we presented in the "Preliminary Remark": It is necessary not only to recognize "against whom" the polemic is directed, but against which specific argument.

We gain a more adequate view of the Nietzschean attack presented here if we read it as a continuation of the polemic against Hegel's *Science of Logic*. In effect, Deleuze has taken the logical attack developed in Bergson and added the question of will—"Who wills a negative ontological movement?" This is the method of dramatization: In Bergson, Deleuze asks the Platonic question "What is the negative logic of being?"; but now, with Nietzsche, he can make the discussion more concrete by dramatizing the investigation in terms of will. We should be careful to keep in mind, though, that the question "Qui?" does not find its answer in an individual, a group, or even a social class; rather, "Qui?" leads us to identify a kind of force, or a specific quality of will. In this dramatization, then, the slave is the persona who plays the will to a negative movement. Nietzsche presents the slave syllogism as the false attempt to arrive at self-affirmation. Once again, even though we are dealing with the question of self-affirmation, the discussion has nothing to do with the subject of consciousness, but rather deals strictly with a logic of valuation dramatized in terms of two personae. The slave plays the negative logic of valuation: "You are evil; therefore I am good." The master's syllogism is the inverse: "I am good; therefore you are evil" (119). Deleuze brilliantly brings this back to the question of logical movement by focusing on the different function of "therefore" in the two cases. In the master's syllogism, the first clause is independent and thus carries the essential, positive statement; "therefore" merely introduces a negative correlate. Master logic appears in Deleuze's description as a sort of efficient causality of valuation—the effect is completely internal to the cause and comes forth through a logical emanation. "Therefore" marks the necessity of an internal movement. In the slave's syllogism, however, "therefore" plays a completely different role; it attempts to reverse the negative first clause to arrive at a positive conclusion. Slave logic tries to operate a completely external movement by using the logical operator "therefore" to relate the two opposite clauses. If we try to pose this logic in causal terms, we find that the slave's "therefore" can only mark a *causa per accidens*. Furthermore, the slave's second clause cannot be a real affirmation because the effect ("I am good") cannot contain more perfection or reality than its cause ("You are evil"). "This is the strange syllogism of the slave: he needs two negations in order to produce an appearance of affirmation" (121). Deleuze is clearly drawing on the Bergsonian logical charges against the negative movement of the dialectic. The affirmation of the slave, like the determination of the dialectic, is a false movement that merely produces a "subsistent exteriority."

While this first Nietzschean attack on slave logic is looking back to Bergson for its foundation (since now will and force have come into play), Deleuze is also able to develop a further, and more powerful, accusation, which looks forward to Spinoza. Negation takes on a different form in the field of forces: The second negation of the slave syllogism (contained in "therefore") is a purely logical negation, whereas the first negation ("You are evil") is a negative *evaluation*. Deleuze explains that the negative value given to the other from the slave perspective is not attributed simply because the other is strong, but because the other does not restrain that strength. This is where Deleuze locates the primary slave paralogism: The initial evaluative negation is based on "the fiction of a force separated from what it can do" (123). The slave logic negates the force of the strong not by opposing it with another force, but by the "fiction" of dividing it into two parts. This fictitious division creates the space for the imputation of evil: It is not evil to be strong, but it is evil to carry that strength into action. The slave's evaluative negation is based on a false conception of the nature of power. The slave maintains that power is a capacity, exterior or transcendent to the field of forces, that can be manifest in action or not. This separation of power into two parts allows for the creation of a "fictitious" causal relationship: "The manifestation is turned into an effect that is referred to the force as if it were a distinct and separated cause" (123). The slave sets up a relationship in which force appears as merely a formal cause—force represents a *possible* manifestation.[2] Nietzsche's master, however, insists that power exists only *en acte* and cannot be separated from its manifestation: "Concrete force is that which goes to its ultimate consequences, to the limit of power or desire" (53). The master conceives an internal, necessary relationship between a force and its manifestation.

What is the reasoning behind Deleuze's claim here? By what logic is slave power merely a "fiction," and master power more real or concrete? Obviously, this cannot be read as simply an empirical observation because Nietzsche would be the first to say that slave power is very real, and, indeed, it is the more prevalent conception in history, to such an extent that "the strong always have to be defended against the weak" (58). To understand this argument, we have to bring it back once again to the ontological plane.[3] As we noted earlier, in Scholastic ontologies the essence of being is its "productivity" and its "producibility," or, in Spinozian terms, power is the essence of being (*Ethics* IP34). Therefore, the slave conception is a "fiction" precisely because it introduces an accidental quality into the power of being by setting up an external causal relation. The master logic provides a more substantial conception of power by posing the effect, the manifestation internal to the cause, that is, internal to being. This evaluation follows from a materialist conception of being, and William Ockham, one of the strictest materialists in the Western tradition, expresses the point clearly:

> The distinction between potential existence [*ens in potentia*] and actual existence [*ens in actu*] ... does not mean that something that is not in the universe, but can exist in the universe, is truly a being, or that something else that is in the universe is also a being. Rather, when Aristotle divides "being" into potentiality and actuality ... he has in mind that the name "being" is predicated of some thing by means of the verb "is," in a proposition that merely states a fact concerning a thing and is not equivalent to a proposition containing the mode of possibility. ... Hence, Aristotle declares in the same place that "being is divisible into potential and actual, as knowledge and rest are"; but nothing is knowing or resting unless it is actually knowing or resting. (*Philosophical Writings* 92)

Ockham's insight leads us directly to the nucleus of Deleuze's Nietzschean distinction between master power and slave power. To say that "the name 'being' is predicated of some thing by means of the verb 'is' " is to say that the power of being is necessarily, efficiently linked to its manifestation, that the force of being is inseparable from "what it can do." The slave's conception of power is a "fiction" because it fails to recognize the real substantial nature of being, and tries to maintain a separation between the potential and the actual through a notion of possibility. Slave power is real and certainly does exist, but it cannot exist as a real expression of substance. The master conception of power reveals being in its actual productivity; in other words, it expresses the essence of being as the actual and efficient (not merely possible or formal) power of being. Framing the discussion in these terms, we can see that Nietzsche's argument has to do not with the quantity of power, but with its quality. "What Nietzsche calls weak or slavish is not the least strong but that which, whatever its strength, is separated from what it can do" (61). The entire discussion of power has little to do with strength or capacity, but with the relation between essence and manifestation, between power and what it can do. What Nietzsche contributes to this discourse on power is an evaluation — he judges the power internal to its manifestation as noble.[4]

This analysis of the nature of power is already very suggestive of an ethics. Deleuze brings out the ethical and political implications of the two types of power with an interesting comparison between Nietzsche and Callicles:

> Callicles strives to distinguish nature and law. Everything that separates a
> force from what it can do he calls law. Law, in this sense, expresses the
> triumph of the weak over the strong. Nietzsche adds: the triumph of
> reaction over action. Indeed, everything that separates a force is reactive
> as is the state of a force separated from what it can do. Every force that
> goes to the limit of its power is, on the contrary, active. It is not a law that
> every force goes to the limit, it is even the opposite of a law. (58-59)

This passage presents a terrain that is very close to that of Spinoza's political writings. First Spinoza affirms that power = virtue = right, and then he opposes *jus* to *lex*. This formulation serves Spinoza as an extension of his ethics and as the foundation for a viable, democratic politics. However, at this point in our reading of Deleuze's Nietzsche, we do not yet have the practical, constructive elements necessary to elaborate this ethical and political terrain. We have a substantial theory of power that can serve as an attack on juridicism (based on the conception of power it implies), but we do yet not have any positive alternative to complement this attack. To fill out this alternative we will have to wait until we can elaborate a conception of ethical practice. For the moment, then, we can only read the Nietzschean analysis of power as suggestive of a future ethics and politics.

We have made great progress in fleshing out the logic and value of Nietzsche's distinction between master power and slave power. However, it is clear that Hegel's master and slave do not tread directly on this same terrain. Hegel's slave is interested in consciousness and independence; he is too preoccupied with his death, and too busy thinking about his work, to pose the question of value.[5] Evidently, the preceding discussion has not been dealing with the *Phenomenology*. Deleuze directs the Nietzschean attack not against Hegel's master and slave, but against an extrapolation from Hegel's *Science of Logic*. We no longer ask the question "What is the dialectical logic of being?" but "Who wills this logic?" This is the line of reasoning that leads us to master and slave valuation and to the two conceptions of power. Thus, Deleuze conducts a second-order critique of Hegel that builds on Bergsonian logic and looks forward to Spinozian politics. We should note that Deleuze's tactics for attacking Hegel have changed somewhat. Even if the rhetoric has intensified, the polemic no longer applies directly to Hegel's argument; it addresses a derivation from Hegel, an implication of his dialectic. This new tactic affords Deleuze a greater autonomy from Hegelian terminology, and, in effect, it transports the dialectic to Deleuze's terrain (in this case, of sense and value) so that he can carry out the combat there.

Remark: The Resurgence of Negativity

A parenthesis about Steven Houlgate's response to Deleuze's charges against slave logic in *Hegel, Nietzsche and the Criticism of Metaphysics* can help us frame the importance of the arguments we have presented. Houlgate's project is to defend Hegel against the recent charges wielded by the French Nietzscheans (Deleuze in particular) and, like a good Hegelian, to go back on the offensive, demonstrating that not only is Hegel invulnerable to Nietzschean critiques, but he actually completes the Nietzschean project better than Nietzsche himself did. He makes two central counterattacks against Deleuze's Nietzscheanism: (1) It fails to appreciate that Hegel's negative logic is required for determination, and (2) its conception of self does not meet the requirements to achieve genuine interiority. Given our reading of the evolution of Deleuze's work and the development of his project, it should be clear that these two points are well off the mark. Houlgate explains:

> Hegel's dialectic is not in fact based upon an initial *external* negation of the specific differences between things, and does not therefore constitute a flight into an abstract world of fictional concepts as Deleuze asserts. . . . According to Hegel's *Science of Logic*, a thing must be *in itself* the negation of something else . . . if it is to have any determinate characteristics . . . at all. The notion of something real or specific that is not negatively determined, or mediated, is precisely what dialectical philosophy shows up to be an impossibility. However, Deleuze fails to see Hegel's point. (7)

"Omnis determinatio est negatio." Houlgate reminds us that if we want determination, we must have negation. Deleuze has shown us in his studies on Bergson that he agrees with this point—but Deleuze is not the one who wants determination. We have seen that the negative movement of determination that founds Hegelian being is, by definition, a completely external movement. Further, when we considered this movement in a causal framework, we found that this external foundation is abstract, that it cannot adequately support being as substance, as *causa sui*. We must admit that Deleuze does not repeat this argument in *Nietzsche and Philosophy*; as we have said, he takes the Bergsonian point for granted and builds on it. However, we have come back to this argument so many times now that it can only appear comical when Houlgate claims that, like Nietzsche, Deleuze does not have an adequate familiarity with Hegel the logician, *doctor subtilis*: "What are the consequences of Deleuze's failure to appreciate Hegel's somewhat rarefied point of logic?" (8). Jean Wahl is much closer to the mark when he claims that Deleuze at times falls into rhetorical exaggerations by giving in to his unbridled hatred for Hegel.[6]

Houlgate's second charge shows a similar confusion of Deleuze's project. He reads Deleuze's Nietzschean critique as if it remained a reformist endeavor, content to criticize Hegel's means, not his ends. Thus, just as Houlgate assumes that Deleuze is striving for determination, which implies negation, so too he assumes as another goal the interiority of self-consciousness, which likewise proves to require negation: "Deleuze thus rules out the possibility that true, concrete selfhood is to be understood in terms of the negation of, or mediation by, the other" (7). And further: "In contrast to Hegel, Deleuze does not believe that genuine self-consciousness requires consciousness of the other's recognition of oneself" (8). Houlgate is assuming that Deleuze's project is to refine or complete Hegel's argument; Deleuze, on the contrary, wants to have nothing to do with self-consciousness and the self it gives rise to (cf. *Nietzsche and Philosophy* 39, 41-42, 80). Along with Nietzsche, he views it as a sickness, a *ressentiment* caused by the reflection of a force back into itself. What Deleuze is searching for, instead, is a productive exteriority that is based on affirmation (36). We can see this point clearly if we keep in mind the implications of Nietzsche's two types of power. Finally, Houlgate shows us one reason why Deleuze might choose not to address directly the master and slave of Hegel's *Phenomenology*: The entire terrain is oriented toward promoting the sickness of interiority and self-consciousness.

2.4 Slave Labor and the Insurrectional Critique

Is it true, as Jean Wahl claims, that there is something richer and more profound in Hegel's analysis of the master-slave dialectic that escapes the Nietzschean critique? Or, on the contrary, has Deleuze already provided us with the weapons for an adequate Nietzschean attack? Let us try to test Deleuze's Nietzschean challenge by bringing it onto Hegel's own terrain. Hegel's slave does not reason, "The master is evil; therefore I am good"; instead, we can pose Hegel's slave syllogism as "I fear death and I am constrained to work; therefore I am an independent self-consciousness." The logic of this syllogism takes two routes—one implicit path in relation to the master, and one explicit path in relation to the object of the slave's labor—which are linked together as a progression to describe the education of the slave.

The implicit path is founded on the slave's confrontation with death, "the absolute Lord." In this encounter, the slave undergoes the negation of everything that is solid and stable in its being: "But this pure universal movement, the absolute melting-away of everything stable, is the simple, essential nature of self-consciousness, absolute negativity, *pure being-for-self* which is *implicit* in this consciousness" (*Phenomenology* §194). On a first consideration, the implicit process seems to develop the following logic: The initial self-consciousness of the slave, a simple being-for-self, is negated in death and then resurrected as an affirmation of life and as a pure being-for-self. However, we cannot understand the logic of this passage unless we note that this "melting-away of everything stable" is not, properly speaking, an absolute or total negation, because it preserves the "essential nature" of the consciousness under siege. The death of the slave would not serve Hegel's purposes: He wants to destroy all that is inessential in the slave, but to stop at the threshold of essence. This partial aggression, this restraint of the destructive force of dialectical negation is what allows for conservation—it is a negation "which supersedes in such a way as to preserve and maintain what is superseded" (§188).

Now, assuming we do accept that it is the opposition (albeit partial) with death that affirms the life of the slave, we can already venture a Bergsonian response to this implicit process. If the difference that animates life is its opposition to death, that is, if the difference of life is absolutely external, then life appears as merely unsubstantial, as a result of chance or hazard, a "subsistent exteriority." Furthermore, when we pose death in general as a contradiction of life in general, we are dealing in terms too imprecise and too abstract to arrive at the singularity and concreteness of the difference that defines real life and subjectivity. In effect, we are dressing life in baggy clothes. Life and death in their abstract opposition are indifferent. Therefore, the affirmation of life that the slave attains "in principle" through the confrontation with death can only be abstract and hollow.

Hegel, however, immediately follows with a response to this challenge: "This moment of pure being-for-self is also *explicit* for the bondsman, for in the lord it exists for him as his *object*. Furthermore, his consciousness is not this dissolution of everything stable merely in principle; in his service he *actually* brings this about" (§194). Here the slave no longer faces "the absolute Lord," abstract death, but he confronts a particular master and is forced to work. This explicit negation takes two forms that are linked together in a progressive movement: a formal negation in the slave's relation to the master, and an actual negation in the slave's relation to his labor. In the master, the slave is confronted by an independent self-consciousness that negates him. However, the slave cannot gain recognition from the master, and thus this form of opposition can only give him "the beginning of wisdom." The second explicit relationship reveals the slave's essential nature, allowing him to become "conscious of what he truly is" (§195). The slave comes out of himself by engaging the thing as object of his labor; he loses or negates himself and finds himself in the thing; finally, he retrieves the essential nature of himself through his negation or transformation of the thing. Through his forced labor, then, the slave negates a specific other (the aspect of himself that has gone out of himself) through working or transforming it, just as the master negates the object of his desire in consuming it. The primary difference between these two negations (master desire and slave labor) lies in the fact that the object of the master's desire appears as a dependent, transitory other, and therefore can provide only fleeting satisfaction; the object of the slave's labor, however, resists his negation, and thus appears as permanent and independent: "Work . . . is desire held in check, fleetingness staved off" (§195). Master desire, like death, is too thorough in its negation for Hegel's purposes: It is the total destruction of the other and the end of the relationship. Work, however, like the near-death Hegel posits in fear, is a "dialectical" or partial negation that allows the "essential nature" of the other to survive and thus perpetuates the relationship. We can understand this entire complex process, from the initial implicit relationship to the final explicit relationship, as the progressive education of the slave. The first moment, the slave's confrontation with death, dissolves the fixity of his life and focuses his attention on the universal (Charles Taylor, *Hegel* 155). This educational fear prepares the slave for his work. Thus prepared, the slave is able, in the second, explicit moment of labor, to achieve his true self-realization: He becomes "conscious of what he truly is."

We should take a moment here to clarify the terms of our reading of this passage. There is a great deal of slippage and ambiguity regarding the level of abstraction and the register of Hegel's argument, which leave it open to a variety of interpretations. It is not clear exactly where we should look to locate the master and the slave—in real individuals? in social classes? in the logical movement of Spirit? What is unclear is the nature of the contents we should attribute to the agents of the drama. Should we read the master-slave dialectic in personalist terms, or rather as an impersonal, logical drama of being? A Hegelian might immediately object to the form of these questions, insisting that Hegel's analysis spans the different registers and effectively unites them in the movement of historical being. Spirit, which is always embodied, is simultaneously the individual subject, the sociohistorical subject, and the essence of being; thus, Hegel's argument slips comfortably between personal and impersonal references, and between microcosm and macrocosm. On this basis, many interpreters invoke a personalist reading to pose the master-slave relation as the affirmation of a liberal ethics of mutual respect that spans both the personal and formal registers: "Men seek and need the recognition of their fellows" (Taylor 152).[7] However, when we refer back to the argument, it is clear that the personalist hypothesis provides certain difficulties for a consistent reading of the text. The master term presents difficulties because, in effect, it can only successfully fit into a personalized mold for brief sections of the analysis. In the implicit half of the passage, the master moves to the extreme extension of its role: "The absolute Lord" is death. This should already indicate to us that the master cannot be read in personal terms. Later in the text, however, the slave discovers his other in the object of his labor, and through his interaction with this object the slave gains the necessary self-recognition. If we read this section as the human need to gain acknowledgment from another human, how could the slave possibly find satisfaction through his relation to the object of his labor? The working slave gains a reflected image of himself from the thing, but never gains acknowledgment from a human or personal other. Indeed, we can only maintain the coherence of the passage if we attribute no personal contents to the master role and read it as an impersonal, logical role or as an objective other. The question remains, however, whether we should read the slave's drama in personal or impersonal terms, as a development of a personal, human consciousness (individual or collective) in an objective world, or as a purely logical development. Let us explore these two possibilities in turn.

If we read the text from a strictly logical perspective, the master-slave drama illustrates the conflict between two forms of negation. The master negation is the villain of the drama because it totally destroys its object and ends the relationship (the master, in its desire/consumption, brings on the death of the other); in contrast, the slave negation is the hero because it operates a partial destruction and perpetuates its object (the slave in its labor). Master negation does not hold back its powers but attacks with full force, while slave negation is the model of restraint: "desire held in check, fleetingness staved off." This is where Deleuze's Nietzsche can finally enter the discussion. Master negation is simply destructive force carried through to its logical conclusion, a force inseparable from its manifestation. Slave negation is force "held in check," that is, restrained from full expression. This is the "fiction" at the essence of slave power. Nietzsche recognizes that this slave negation is the reflective moment of self-consciousness, the interiorization of force: "Whatever the reason that an active force is falsified, deprived of its conditions of operation and separated from what it can do, *it is turned back inside, turned back against itself*" (*Nietzsche and Philosophy* 127-28). This is perfectly coherent with the Hegelian argument. The essence of the slave that emerges victoriously from the dialectic is the universal essence of being: pure self-consciousness. Interiority is the essence of Hegelian being. Here we can see Hegel and Nietzsche on the same terrain, marching in precisely opposite directions. Both seek to locate essence in the movement of being, but Hegel discovers a force reflected back into itself (self-consciousness or interiority), and Nietzsche proposes a force that emerges unhaltingly outside itself (the will to power or exteriority). The discussion comes back once again to the nature of power. If, in both cases, the essence of being is power, they are two radically different conceptions of power. Our terms are clumsy, but the distinction is clear: On one side, there is power separated from what it can do, Hegelian reflection, Ockham's *ens in potentia*, or Spinoza's *potestas*; on the other side, there is power internal to its manifestation, Ockham's *ens in actu* and Spinoza's *potentia*. We have seen that a modified Scholastic argument is available to Deleuze to defend the "efficient" conception of power in logical terms. Here, however, Deleuze follows Nietzsche's argument and shows a series of negative practical effects that are consequent on this slave victory of interiority, such as pain, guilt, and sin (*Nietzsche and Philosophy* 128-31). Once again we can see why Deleuze might choose not to address Hegel's master-slave dialectic directly, because the entire discussion is directed toward self-consciousness, toward interiority, a condition antithetical to joy and affirmation.

Furthermore, in these same logical terms and in a perfectly coherent fashion, the "education" of the slave reveals a critical method of partial negations. The first moment of the critique is the slave's close confrontation with, or fear of, death; this moment is the *pars destruens*, but it is a limited *pars destruens* since the "essential nature" of the slave is spared. This confrontation purports to free the slave from the fixity of its previously stable conditions and allows it to operate the second moment of the critique, the *pars construens*, through the slave's labor. This second moment, however, is not properly a *pars construens*. It is not really productive, but rather revelatory; the slave is not created or substantially transformed in this second moment, but rather "becomes conscious of what he truly is" (195). Charles Taylor's term for this moment of labor—a "standing negation"—is adequate because it shows that there is really no progression here. Posed in these logical terms, then, we can finally make good on Deleuze's claim cited earlier that it is precisely the errors of the Kantian critique that lead to the Hegelian dialectic. Like the Kantian critique, the dialectical critique described by the education of the slave is neither total nor positive. The partiality of its destructive moment spares precisely what takes the place of creation in the productive moment, the "essential nature" of the slave. However, while Kant "seems to have confused the positivity of critique with a humble recognition of the rights of the criticised" (*Nietzsche and Philosophy* 89), this Hegelian slave critique has made the criticized into the hero of the drama. The triumph of this dialectical critique is that the essential nature of the slave survives and is revealed in pure form in a stable configuration of partial, "standing" negations. Only the master's active negation, the unrestrained attack, the death of the adversary can lead to a total critique, and therefore to the opportunity for a positive, original creation: "Destruction as the active destruction of the man who wants to perish and to be overcome announces the creator" (178). The differences between the two types of power, then, are directly related to the two types of critique. Nietzsche's master power, in which force is internal to its manifestation, knows no restraint and thus operates a total critique; when power is separated from what it can do, on the other hand, the *pars destruens* that initiates the critique can only be partial.

All of this we have discovered by reading Hegel's argument as if the slave were an impersonal force playing out a logical position. However, if we are to emphasize the educational journey of the slave as the development of a particular self-consciousness, as Hegel does, it seems that we have to fill the slave with some general personal contents. What exactly is the "essential nature" of the slave that survives the onslaught of critical forces and emerges victorious from the development? Hegel would have us believe that the slave essence is content-less as pure self-consciousness, and that this essence is not particular to the slave, but is the very essence of being. The coherence of Hegel's argument, however, relies on the differential *relationship* between the slave and its master. The movement that defines and reveals essence cannot develop with any actor, but is dependent on a specific position in the relationship. We see, of course, that the master does not embody this movement. Since the logic of the drama turns on the slave's position in the relationship, the essence of the slave has to involve his servitude.[8] The first moment of the critique (the fear of death, the relation to the master) makes the slave more intent on its activity, and the second moment (work) is its pure expression. It is precisely slave labor that survives and is purified through the critical education. The text makes clear, however, that the work of the slave cannot be considered as creative energy or productive force; on the contrary, the slave's work is fundamentally his role in a "standing" relationship.

The tradition of Marxist thought has known all too many interpretations that (directly or indirectly) exalt this Hegelian proposition: The worker occupies an exalted position because his or her work expresses human essence. Thus, the history of the workers' struggle becomes an educational drama that assaults, "melting away," the inessential character of the worker in order to affirm the essential nature of work. The worker is liberated inasmuch as work is affirmed as his or her essence. This is the Stakhanovite "dignity" of the worker. Marx will have no part of this: Leave it to the bosses to sing the praises of work. What is at issue here is not the description of the worker's existence in a relationship, but the proposition that this role constitutes the *essence* of the worker. Marx makes a perfectly analogous argument in relation to the State: "Hegel is not to be blamed because he describes the existence of the Modern State such as it is, but because he passes off what it is as the *essence of the State*" ("Critique of Hegel's Philosophy of Right" 63). This is where we can see Deleuze's Nietzsche and Marx very close to one another, in an unrestrained attack on the essence of established values. They both conceive of real essence not as work, but as a force: power, the will to power, living labor, creation.[9] But in order to liberate that force, to provide the room for the *pars construens*, the constructive, transformative force, they must both conduct a radical, total critique, an unlimited *pars destruens*, attacking the essence of the established values. If the worker is to reach a point of genuine affirmation, of self-valorization, the attack has to be directed at the "essence," at the values that define the worker as such—against servitude, against work.[10] In this context, Nietzsche appears in the position of Marxist workerism: "In order to struggle against capital, the working class must struggle against itself inasmuch as it is capital. ... Workers' struggle against work, struggle of the worker against himself inasmuch as worker" (Tronti 260). The worker attacking work, attacking himself inasmuch as worker, is a beautiful means of understanding Nietzsche's "man who wants to perish and to be overcome." In attacking himself, he is attacking the relationship that has been posed as his essence—only after this "essence" is destroyed can he truly be able to create. A Hegelian partial critique is at best a reformism, preserving the essence of what it attacks—it "supersedes in such a way as to preserve and maintain what is superseded" (*Phenomenology* §188). A total critique is necessarily an insurrectional critique. And only that unrestrained destruction of established "essence" can allow for genuine creation. Deleuze's Nietzsche appears as a prophet of what Lenin calls "the art of insurrection."[11]

Remark: The Will to Workers' Power and the Social Synthesis

Is *Nietzsche and Philosophy* an untimely hymn to the workers of '68? Through Deleuze's reading, we have found a surprisingly strong confluence between Nietzsche and Marx (and even Lenin) in terms of the power, the radicality, and the creativity of the practical critique. However, we are not prepared here to confront the Nietzsche-Marx question in all its complexity. In this "Remark," I wish only to touch on the question, somewhat indirectly, by considering Deleuze's Nietzschean arguments in terms of Nanni Balestrini's *Vogliamo tutto* (We want everything), a simple, beautiful Italian novel that recounts the story of a worker at the FIAT plant in the late 1960s and his involvement in the formation of the political movement *Potere operaio* (Workers' Power).[12] What interests me initially in this comparison is the radical attack on the established notion of essence as a precondition for change and creation. In Nietzschean terms, Deleuze often expresses this as the attack on "man" or as a moment in the effort to go beyond man, to create new terms and values of human existence (*Nietzsche and Philosophy* 64-65; also *Foucault* 131-41). This is the same notion expressed by the workers' "refusal of work," an attack against their established essence so as to be able to create new terms of existence. Note that the workers' refusal is not only a refusal *to* work but a refusal *of* work, that is, a refusal of a specific existing relation of production. In other words, the workers' attack on work, their violent *pars destruens*, is directed precisely at their own essence.

In the first section of *Vogliamo tutto*, the protagonist cannot yet pose his desires in such political terms; nonetheless, what he hates most of all is precisely what defines his social existence and what is presented to him as his essence. Thus, he cannot understand why anyone would want to celebrate work on May Day: "What a joke to celebrate labor day. . . . I never understood why work ought to be celebrated" (74). Workers who accept the established value of work appear to him as closed, blocked from what they can do, and it is precisely this acceptance of the established values as essence that makes them dangerous: "Thick people obtuse without the least bit of imagination dangerous. Not fascists just obtuse. Those in the PCI [Italian Communist Party] were bread and work. I was a '*qualunquista*' [nonideological, value-less] at least I was recuperable. But they completely accepted work and for them work was everything" (85-86). Those who accept "bread and work" as their essence as workers are unable to imagine, unable to create. The danger they present is that of a forced stasis, a deadening of creative powers, and a perpetuation of the established essence. In this context, a *"qualunquista"* is already in a better position. The lack of values, of beliefs, provides a space on which imagination and creation can act. From this position, from the recognition of his antagonism toward work as a relation of production, the protagonist begins a progressively more political attack on work itself. Thus far, we are still on the terrain of Deleuze's Nietzsche, with the total critique of established values. Here we have a developed example of the worker attacking work, and therefore attacking himself inasmuch as worker—a beautiful instance of Nietzsche's "man who wants to perish," the active and liberatory destruction that must be distinguished from the passivity of the "last man," the PCIista who completely accepts work (cf. *Nietzsche and Philosophy* 174).

The protagonist of *Vogliamo tutto*, however, only gains the real power to carry out this destructive project when he begins to recognize his commonality with the other workers. The voice of the narrative takes on a continually broader scope, shifting from first person singular to first person plural as the mass of workers begin to recognize what they can do and what they can become: "All the stuff all the wealth we produce is ours. . . . We want everything. All the wealth all the power and no work" (128). The expansion of the collective expression is matched by an expansion of the will. It is precisely the wealth of the collectivity that provides the basis for the violent radicality of critique: "What began to come up was the desire to struggle not because the work not because the boss were bad but because they exist. What began to come out was the demand to want power, in short" (128). The recognition of collective desires goes hand in hand with the development and expansion of collective practice. The workers' strikes build to the point where they spill outside of the factory as demonstrations in the streets and violent conflict involving large parts of the city. Finally, this collective destructive expression, this moment of intense violence, opens the possibility for the subsequent joy and creation: "But now the thing that moved them more than anger was joy. The joy of being finally strong. Of discovering that these demands that this struggle were the demands of everyone that it was the struggle of everyone" (171). This is the climax of the novel, the point where the struggle transforms from a *pars destruens* driven by hatred for the bosses and work to a *pars construens* of workers' joy in feeling their power. In this focal point, the struggle is converted from negation to affirmation. This is the hour of "midnight," Nietzsche's transmutation (*Nietzsche and Philosophy* 171-75). The workers' attack on their essence as workers arrives at a moment when they are able to "go beyond," to discover a terrain of creation and joy beyond the "worker."

I would like to emphasize two elements of this workers' transmutation. The first is that the entire critical movement is necessarily tied to a broadening movement of the collectivity. The workers' recognition of their commonality and their expression in collective action take the form of a spatial or social *synthesis*, composing an expansive and coherent body of desire: As the body of workers expands, their will and power grow. The synthesis involved in the workers' collectivity is an eternal return of the will not in time but in space, the return of the will laterally throughout the mass of workers. It would be a poor formulation to say that the workers are powerful because they come together—this would imply a calculation of individual sacrifice for achieving extrinsic collective goods. Rather, the workers' power and their joy lie precisely in the fact that they will and act together. The workers form a powerful assemblage. The second element I would like to emphasize is that the transmutation comes about through the *practice* of the workers. Precisely when the workers "actualize" their critique, when they pass into action in the factory and in the streets, they achieve the constructive moment of joy and creation. The "actualization" of the workers is a practice of joy. These two elements give us the terms for the remainder of our study of Deleuze's Nietzsche: How does Nietzsche conceive a real synthesis of forces, and how do these forces manifest themselves in terms of practice?

2.5 The Being of Becoming: The Ethical Synthesis of the Efficient Will

When Deleuze approaches the question of a Nietzschean synthesis, he comes back once again to the affirmation of multiplicity and the attack on the dialectic. "Hegel wanted to ridicule pluralism" (*Nietzsche and Philosophy* 4): The dialectic of the One and the Multiple sets up a false image of multiplicity that is easily recuperable in the unity of the One. We have treated this charge at some length in the second phase of Bergson study (Section 1.3). As we have seen, the most potent Bergsonian attack against the dialectic in this regard is the construction of a veritable multiplicity, of differences of nature. We find this same attack in Deleuze's Nietzsche: "Pluralism sometimes appears to be dialectical—but it is its most ferocious enemy, its only profound enemy" (8). Pluralism or multiplicity is so dangerous for the dialectic precisely because it is irreducible to unity. Through the analysis of Bergson's work, Deleuze brings out the irreducibility and eminence of multiplicity in clear, logical terms; but, as we have seen, in this context Deleuze only succeeds in posing the complementary moment of the organization of the Multiple in very weak terms. Indeed, it seems that the irreducibility of the multiplicity prohibits any idea of organization. We have argued that the failure to provide an adequate notion of organization is what makes Deleuze's Bergson most vulnerable to a Hegelian counter-attack. This is where Nietzsche provides Deleuze with an enormous advance.

"The game has two moments that are those of the dicethrow—the dice that is thrown and the dice that falls back" (25). The two moments of the dicethrow constitute the basic elements of Nietzsche's alternative to the dialectic of the One and the Multiple. The first moment of the game is the easier to understand. The throw of the dice is the affirmation of chance and multiplicity precisely because it is the refusal of control: Just as we saw in the Bergson studies, this is not the multiplicity of order; there is nothing preformed in the possibility of this moment—it is the indeterminate, the unforeseeable. This is Bergson's creative evolution (or emanation) of being, and in Nietzschean terms this is the becoming of being: pure multiplicity. The moment that the dice fall back, however, is more obscure and more complex: "The dice that are thrown once are the affirmation of *chance*, the combination that they form on falling is the affirmation of *necessity*. Necessity is affirmed of chance in exactly the same sense that being is affirmed of becoming and unity is affirmed of multiplicity" (26). The falling back of the dice is not merely a confirmation of the necessity of the given, of multiple reality; this would merely be a determinism, and it would risk negating rather than affirming the first moment of the game. Instead, the falling back of the dice is a moment of the organization of unity—it is not the passive revelation, but the active creation of being. To understand this, we have to relate the dicethrow metaphor to the eternal return:

> The dice that fall back necessarily affirm the number or the destiny that
> brings the dice back. ... The eternal return is the second moment, the
> result of the dicethrow, the affirmation of necessity, the number that
> *brings together all the parts of chance*. But it is also the return of the first
> moment, the repetition of the dicethrow, the reproduction and
> reaffirmation of chance itself. (27-28, emphasis mine)

The dicethrow metaphor is admittedly somewhat strained at this point, but we must recognize the second moment as a moment of organization that constructs unity, that constitutes being by bringing together "all the parts of chance" created in the first moment—not according to any preformed order, but in an original organization. The return of the dice is an affirmation of the dicethrow in that it constitutes the original elements of chance in a coherent whole. Not only does the first moment (of multiplicity and becoming) imply the second moment (of unity and being), but this second moment is also the return of the first: The two moments imply one another as a perpetual series of shattering and gathering, as a centrifugal moment and a centripetal moment, as emanation and constitution.

What is the logic of the synthesis or constitution of being in the eternal return? We can no longer pose this question on a purely logical plane; Nietzsche has transformed the terrain, so that we can only consider such ontological questions in terms of force and value:

> The synthesis is one of forces, of their difference and their reproduction; the eternal return is the synthesis that has as its principle the will to power. We should not be surprised by the word "will"; *which one* apart from the will is capable of serving as the principle of a synthesis of forces by determining the relation of force with forces? (50)

We have seen from the outset that the will is the dynamic that moves and animates the horizon of force and value: The logic of the synthesis, then, is the logic of the will. The will to power is the principle of the synthesis that marks the being of becoming, the unity of the multiplicity and the necessity of chance. How, though, does the will provide a foundation for being? We are not so far from the Scholastic horizon that we earlier drew on so heavily. In effect, the will to power is the principle of the eternal return in that it plays the role of a primary cause, defining the necessity and substantiality of being. Nietzsche's terrain, however, quickly transforms this logical/ontological point into an ethics. The eternal return of the will is an ethics inasmuch as it is a "selective ontology" (72).[13] It is selective because not every will returns: Negation comes only once; only affirmation returns. The eternal return is the selection of the affirmative will as being. Being is not given in Nietzsche; being must be willed. In this sense, ethics comes before ontology in Nietzsche. The ethical will is the will that returns; the ethical will is the will that wills being. This is the sense in which the eternal return is a temporal synthesis of forces: It demands that the will to power wills unity in time. Deleuze formulates the ethical selection of the eternal return as a practical rule for the will: "Whatever you will, will it in such a way that you also will its eternal return" (68). We should note here, however, that when we read Deleuze's rule of the eternal return, we must be careful not to emphasize the word "also." This "also" can be very misleading because the eternal return is not separate from the will, but internal to it. "How does the eternal return perform the selection here? It is the *thought* of the eternal return that selects. It makes willing something whole" (69). The ethical will is whole, internal to its return: "Always do what you will" (*Nietzsche and Philosophy* 69, quoted from *Thus Spake Zarathustra* 191). The principle of the eternal return as being is the efficient will as an ethical will.

We can now trace a beautiful trajectory of this fundamental idea of effi-
ciency and internality: from the logical centrality of efficient difference (the
difference internal to the thing), to the ontological centrality of efficient
power (the force internal to its manifestation), and now to the ethical centrality of the efficient will, the principle of the eternal return. A Scholastic
logic runs through this series as the guiding thread, providing it a materialist, metaphysical foundation: The internal nature of the cause to its effect
is what supports the necessity, substantiality, singularity, and univocity of
being. This is how we can understand the eternal return of the efficient will
as the ethical pillar of a Nietzschean philosophy of being. We asked ourselves earlier, in our analysis of Deleuze's work on Bergson (Section 1.3)
how a philosophy of "indetermination" can also be a philosophy of being,
how we can have both becoming and being. Here we have a Nietzschean
answer. The dicethrow (the moment of becoming, of indetermination) is
followed by dice falling back (the selection of being), which in turn leads
to a new dicethrow. The ontological selection does not negate the indetermination of the dicethrow, but enhances it, affirms it, just as the eternal
return is an affirmation of the will.

Finally, pure being is attained in Nietzsche as an achieved state, a finality,
and it is presented in the persona of Ariadne. The love of Ariadne for
Dionysus is the affirmation of the eternal return; it is a double affirmation,
the raising of the being of becoming to its highest power. Dionysus is the
god of affirmation, but it takes Ariadne to affirm affirmation itself: "Eternal
affirmation of being, eternally I am your affirmation" (187, quoted from
Dionysian Dithyrambs). Dionysus's affirmation marks the being of becoming; therefore, since Ariadne takes Dionysus for the object of her affirmation, she marks the pure affirmation of being. Ariadne's affirmation is a
double affirmation ("the 'yes' that responds to 'yes' " ["Mystère d'Ariane"
15]), or, more properly, it is a spiraling, infinite affirmation—affirmation
raised to the nth power. Ariadne's creation of pure being is an ethical act,
an act of love.

2.6 The Total Critique as the Foundation of Being

On this ethical terrain of the efficient, affirmative will, Deleuze reproposes
the drama of the total critique, one last time, now in terms of valuation—as
"transmutation." Deleuze presents the critique this time through a combination of refurbished Kantian and Scholastic terms. In effect, transmutation
moves from Kantianism to Scholasticism in that it moves from a critique of
knowledge to a foundation of being.[14] Here, also, we find Deleuze's final
attack on the Hegelian dialectic, albeit in distant, indirect form. As we have

already seen, the standpoint of the critique, free from its transcendental instance, is the will to power. Now the antagonistic moment, the *pars destruens* of the critique, is played by nihilism. Deleuze explains that nihilism is the *ratio cognoscendi* of the will to power: "What we in fact *know* of the will to power is suffering and torture" (173, emphasis mine). Deleuze has explained at great length that nihilism, as a project of interiority and consciousness, is full of pain and suffering; however, this same nihilism is what reveals "all the values known or knowable up to the present" (172). We gain knowledge of ourselves and our present through the suffering of the negative will to power. As Kant has taught us, though, there is a beyond to this knowledge: "We 'think' the will to power in a form distinct from that in which we know it. (Thus the *thought* of the eternal return goes beyond all the laws of our *knowledge*.)" (172-73). Nihilism itself is what takes us beyond interiority, beyond suffering: The power of the negative in this critique does not operate a Hegelian "standing negation"; instead, this "completed" nihilism is an *active* will to nothingness—"self-destruction, active destruction" (174). Completed nihilism is self-destruction in two senses: Completion means that nihilism defeats itself so that the final act of the negative will to power is to extinguish itself; also, the completion of nihilism is the end of "man" as a constructed interiority—it is the suicide of the "last man."

At the limit of this destruction, at midnight, the focal point, there is a transformation, a conversion from knowledge to creation, from savage negation to absolute affirmation, from painful interiority to joyful exteriority: "The legislator takes the place of the 'scholar,' *creation takes the place of knowledge itself* and affirmation takes the place of all negations" (173). Affirmation, the *pars construens* of the will to power, is "the unknown joy, the unknown happiness, the unknown God" (173) that is beyond the *ratio cognoscendi*. With the active completion of nihilism and the transmutation to affirmation and creation, we are finally finished with negativity, interiority, and consciousness as such. Exteriority is the condition for the grounding of being: The *ratio essendi* of the will to power, Deleuze explains, is affirmation. These terms allow Deleuze to reformulate a statement of Zarathustra as an ontological ethics: "I love the one who makes use of nihilism as the *ratio cognoscendi* of the will to power, but who finds in the will to power a *ratio essendi* in which man is overcome and therefore nihilism is defeated" (174). Being is primary over knowledge. Like Ariadne, Zarathustra loves being, the creation and affirmation of being. Exteriority, affirmation, the efficient will to power: This is the *ratio* that supports being, and this is what Zarathustra loves.

Remark: The End of Deleuze's Anti-Hegelianism

We noted at the outset of this chapter that one of the central goals in Deleuze's study of Nietzsche is to flesh out an alternative to dialectical opposition that would be an "opposition to the dialectic itself" (17). It is precisely the dialectic's ability to recuperate opposition that is often used to critique contemporary anti-Hegelians such as Deleuze. Judith Butler forcefully poses the question of an opposition to Hegelianism in *Subjects of Desire*: "What constitutes the latest stage of post-Hegelianism as a stage definitively beyond the dialectic? Are these positions still haunted by the dialectic, even as they claim to be in utter opposition to it? What is the nature of this 'opposition,' and is it perchance a form that Hegel himself has prefigured?" (176). Butler answers these questions in strictly Hegelian fashion: "References to a 'break' with Hegel are almost always impossible, if only because Hegel has made the very notion of 'breaking with' into the central tenet of the dialectic" (183-84). From this perspective, opposition itself is essentially dialectical, and hence "opposition to the dialectic itself" can only mean a reinforcement or repetition of the dialectic. In other words, any effort to be an "other" to Hegelianism can be effectively recuperated as an "other" within Hegelianism.

Through our reading of Deleuze's Nietzsche we have explored two points that could constitute adequate responses to Butler's proposition. Deleuze's elaboration of the total critique provides us a direct response by showing that there are two different types of opposition. Dialectical opposition is a restrained, partial attack that seeks to "preserve and maintain" its enemy; it is a sort of low-intensity warfare that can be prolonged indefinitely in a "standing negation." In effect, the dialectic pillages and reforms the essence of its predecessor through a partial critique. Therefore, the "breaking with" that is a central tenet of the dialect can only be a partial rupture, preserving the continuity that characterizes the prefix "post." Nondialectical opposition, however, is that which operates a complete rupture with its opponent through an unrestrained, savage attack. The result of this profound opposition is a separation that prohibits the recuperation of relations. It would be a mistake, then, to call this Nietzschean position "post-Hegelian," as if it built on, reformed, or completed Hegelianism. Deleuze's claim is that the Nietzschean total critique is a "post-Kantian" position — it corrects the Kantian errors to realize the goals of Kant's own original project. Kant's critique allows established values to persist on the transcendental plane as essence. This exception is a result of Kant's incompleteness, and this is the fundamental error that Nietzsche corrects. In Hegel's dialectical critique, however, the established values that are posed as essence are presented as the central protagonist of the critical drama. It is impossible to conceive of the Nietzschean total critique and its unrestrained *pars destruens* as a reform of this position—it can only appear as a profound rupture. At this point, we can clearly see the need for Deleuze's care in positioning the relation to proximate and fundamental enemies. Deleuze's Nietzsche can appear as "post-Kantian" but only "anti-Hegelian": The difference is between reform and rupture. Posed in historiographic terms, Butler's Hegelian claim is that there are only continuous lines in the history of philosophy, reformed to a greater or lesser extent as differences of degree. Deleuze, on the contrary, insists that the history of philosophy contains real discontinuities, veritable differences of nature, and that discontinuity is the only way of posing the Hegel-Nietzsche relationship: "There is no possible compromise between Hegel and Nietzsche" (195).

Deleuze offers us, however, a second response. As we have proceeded through the evolution of Deleuze's thought we have seen the terrain on which he can address Hegelianism constantly shrinking, and we have seen that his attacks on the dialectic have become more and more indirect. The Bergsonian attack on the One and the Multiple, and the Nietzschean attack on the master-slave relation, are carried out on planes completely removed from Hegel's discourse. Deleuze's strategy of developing a total opposition to the dialectic is accompanied by another strategy: to move away from the dialectic, to forget the dialectic. We have arrived at the end of Deleuze's anti-Hegelianism. Even though rhetoric against the dialectic will reappear, in the opening of *Différence et répétition*, for example, it is only to repeat the arguments developed in these early studies, not to develop new ones. The development of a total opposition to the dialectic seems to have been an intellectual cure for Deleuze: It has exorcised Hegel and created an autonomous plane for thought, one that is no longer anti-Hegelian, but that, quite simply, has forgotten the dialectic.

2.7 Pathos and Joy: Toward a Practice of Affirmative Being

A philosophy of joy is necessarily a philosophy of practice. Throughout Deleuze's reading of Nietzsche we have the impression that practice plays a central role, but the terms never come out clearly. It is very clear, on the other hand, what Deleuze's Nietzsche is not: It is not an investigation of consciousness; it is not only a reformation of the understanding or an emendation of the intellect; in short, it is not the construction of an interiority, but a creation of exteriority through the power of affirmation. The exteriority of thought and of the will, however, is not yet an adequate characterization, because Nietzschean affirmation is also corporeal. We have one last passage to make in our reading of Deleuze's Nietzsche: from will to appetite and desire, from exteriority to practice.

Deleuze's elaboration of Nietzschean exteriority rediscovers a Spino-zian proposition: "Will to power is manifested as a power to be affected [pouvoir d'être affecté]" (62, modified).[15] Spinoza conceives a positive re-lation between a body's power to be affected and its power to effect (see Section 3.7): "The more ways a body could be affected the more force it had" (62). Two aspects of this Spinozian conception interest Deleuze in the context of Nietzsche's work. First, this power to be affected never deals with a possibility, but it is always actualized in relations with other bodies. Second, this power defines the receptivity of a body not as a passivity, but as "an *affectivity*, a sensibility, a sensation" (62). What this notion affords Deleuze is a means of posing inner experience as a mode of corporeal exteriority. The receptivity of a body is closely tied to its active external ex-pression: Affectivity is an attribute of the body's power. In Nietzsche, as in Spinoza, then, pathos does not involve a body "suffering" passions; on the contrary, pathos involves the affects that mark the activity of the body, the creation that is joy.

To arrive at a practical conception of joy, however, this rich sense of the power of the affectivity of bodies must be accompanied by an elaboration of the activity of bodies in practice. The very last section of *Nietzsche and Philosophy* approaches this problem:

> Nietzsche's practical teaching is that difference is happy; that multiplicity,
> becoming and chance are adequate objects of joy by themselves and that
> only joy returns. . . . Not since Lucretius has the critical enterprise that
> characterizes philosophy been taken so far (with the exception of
> Spinoza). Lucretius exposes the trouble of the soul and those who need it
> to establish their power—Spinoza exposes sorrow, all the causes of
> sorrow and all those who found their power at the heart of this sorrow—
> Nietzsche exposes *ressentiment*, bad conscience and the power of the
> negative that serves as their principle. (190)

This history of practical philosophies of joy (Lucretius, Spinoza, Nietzsche) is very suggestive. However, in Deleuze's Nietzsche there are two elements that block the development of a practical struggle against the sad passions: elements that direct us forward to the study of Spinoza. First, Deleuze's "impersonal" reading of Nietzsche blocks the development of a theory of practice because it limits our conception of agents to the interplay of forces. We have noted that when Deleuze asks the question "Qui?" he avoids all "personalist" references, and looks rather to a specific will to power. At this point, however, we need to look not only to the will, but also to the appetite and desire.[16] The attributes of a practical agent must be "personalist" in some sense—for a theory of practice we do not need an individualist theory, but we do need a corporeal and desiring agent.

Spinoza is exemplary in this regard when he defines the agent of practice, the "Individual," as a body or group of bodies recognized for its common movement, its common behavior, its common desire (*Ethics* IIP13Def). A corporeal agent such as Spinoza's can lead a struggle against the sad passions and discover a practice of joy. Second, Deleuze's study of Nietzsche fails to arrive at a theory of practice because it does not arrive at a conception of a spatial or social synthesis. The Nietzschean synthesis, the eternal return, is a temporal synthesis that projects the will to power in time. Spinoza will show us, however, that a practice of joy takes place on the plane of sociality: Spinoza's common notions, for example, provide the terms for an expansive collectivity, for the creation of society, and thus constitute a powerful weapon against the sad passions. This final section of *Nietzsche and Philosophy*, then, is already looking forward to the next passage in Deleuze's evolution: from Nietzschean affirmation to Spinozian practice.

Chapter 3

Spinozian Practice
Affirmation and Joy

One can recognize immediately that Deleuze's reading of Spinoza has a different quality than his treatment of other philosophers. There is a certain modesty and caution before Spinoza that we do not find elsewhere. We should keep in mind, of course, that Deleuze presented *Expressionism in Philosophy: Spinoza* as the historical portion of his doctoral thesis, but this fact can only provide a partial explanation for the change in tone. As we have seen, Deleuze often presents his investigations in the history of philosophy in the form of extreme simplicity, as the elaboration of a single idea: ontological positivity for Bergson, ethical affirmation for Nietzsche. These studies take the form of clean-cut jewels. They pose the essential idea from which an entire philosophical doctrine follows. In comparison, Deleuze's work on Spinoza is very ragged; it is spilling over with underdeveloped insights and unresolved problems. Precisely for this reason it is a more open work, and at the same time a work that is less accessible to a general public.[1] *Expressionism in Philosophy: Spinoza* appears as a set of working notes that do not present a completed interpretation, but rather propose a series of interpretative strategies in the process of development. Therefore, the theoretical passages that we will follow here are necessarily complex, and often elliptical:

> It was on Spinoza that I worked the most seriously according to the
> norms of the history of philosophy—but it was Spinoza more than any
> other that gave me the feeling of a gust of air that pushes you on the back

each time you read him, a witch's broomstick that he mounts you atop.
We have not yet begun to understand Spinoza, and I myself no more than
others. (*Dialogues* 15)

Spinoza remains an enigma.

Our task is to discern how the reading of Spinoza contributes to the
development and evolution of Deleuze's project. Let us go back to our initial methodological principles. We presented as a hypothesis at the outset,
and we have confirmed in our first two chapters, that there is an evolution
in Deleuze's early thought. His historical monographs approach the work
of the individual philosophers according to the demands of his own intellectual project. With Bergson, Deleuze develops an ontology. With Nietzsche, he sets that ontology in motion to constitute an ethics. With Spinoza,
we will take a further step in this evolution, toward politics, building a new
wing onto the structure of a Bergsonian ontology and a Nietzschean ethics.
A particular and important aspect of Deleuze's evolution is that it does not
involve exchanging one theoretical perspective for another, but rather it is
a process of accumulation and constitution. In other words, each step, each
new terrain of investigation, is a construction that never abandons or negates, but rather reproposes the terms of its predecessor. Deleuze carries
his baggage with him. Nietzschean ethics is Bergsonian ontology transported to the field of value; Spinozian politics is Bergsonian ontology and
Nietzschean ethics transported to the field of practice. Ontology inheres in
ethics, which in turn inheres in politics. Spinoza's politics is an ontological
politics in that, through a rich analysis of power and a conceptual elaboration of practice, the principles that animate being are the very same principles that animate an ethics and a practical constitution of political organization.

In the study of Spinoza, however, Deleuze does not immediately proceed beyond his previous results; rather, he takes a few steps back in order
to prepare the leap ahead. In effect, in Deleuze's reading of Spinoza we can
find a summary of the entire evolution. In the first half of his study, corresponding roughly to his reading of the first two books of the *Ethics*, we find
a reelaboration of the terrain that he treated in his study of Bergson (the
plenitude of being, the positivity of difference, the problem of emanation,
etc.); in the second half of Deleuze's reading, treating the final books of the
Ethics, we find a reworking and extension of the Nietzschean terrain (the
affirmation of being, the ethics of power and activity, etc.). Bergson and
Nietzsche breathe life into Spinoza, standing as his primary predecessors:
In Deleuze's inverted history of philosophy, Spinoza seems to be able to
look back and see that he too is not alone on the mountaintops.[2]

Our focus on this Deleuzian evolution allows us to recognize another thesis that is important in the context of Spinoza studies. Throughout *Expressionism in Philosophy: Spinoza*, we can see that Deleuze treats the Spinozian system as two distinct moments, as two perspectives of thought, one speculative and another practical. This distinction between speculation and practice, which remains implicit in Deleuze's work, is both a theoretical claim and an interpretative strategy. In other words, although Deleuze does not highlight this distinction, we can see that it clearly constitutes a challenge to the traditional commentaries on Spinozian thought. For example, Ferdinand Alquié, one of the most acute readers, maintains that, unlike Descartes, Spinoza is not a "philosopher of method" who starts from the human point of view to build toward a divine perspective, but rather a "philosopher of system" setting out directly from the point of view of God: The *Ethics* is principally a systematic, rather than a methodological, text (*Nature et vérité* 34). Deleuze, however, presents the *Ethics* as a double text that proceeds from both of the perspectives identified by Alquié: The first moment of the *Ethics*, speculative and analytic, proceeds in the centrifugal direction from God to the thing in order to discover and express the principles that animate the system of being; the second moment of the *Ethics*, practical and synthetic, moves in the centripetal direction from the thing to God by forging an ethical method and a political line of conduct. The two moments are fundamentally linked: The moment of research, the *Forschung*, prepares the terrain for the moment of presentation and practice, the *Darstellung*. The two moments cover the same terrain of being, but from different perspectives. One of the important consequences of recognizing these two moments of Spinoza's thought, as we will see, is that there are substantial nuances in Spinoza's major concepts (universal, absolute, adequate, necessary, rational, etc.) when one considers them from one perspective or the other. In reading Deleuze's previous works, we have insisted at length on the importance of his critical procedure: *pars destruens, pars construens*. Here we are presented with a similar procedure, but the moment of opposition, of antagonism, of destruction, has changed. We still find a Deleuzian opposition in *Expressionism in Philosophy: Spinoza* (to Descartes, to Leibniz, to the Scholastics, etc.), but this opposition no longer plays a foundational role. Rather than a destructive moment followed by a constructive moment, Deleuze's Spinoza presents a speculative, logical investigation followed by a practical, ethical constitution: *Forschung* followed by *Darstellung*. The two moments, then, speculation and practice, are fundamentally linked, but they remain autonomous and distinct—each with its own method and animating spirit. "The sense of joy appears as the properly ethical sense; it is to practice what affirmation itself is to speculation. . . . A philosophy of pure affirmation, the *Ethics* is also a philosophy of the joy corresponding to such affirmation" (*Expressionism in Philosophy: Spinoza* 272, modified). The affirmation of speculation and the joy of practice are the two threads that weave together to form the general design of the *Ethics*.

Continually in Deleuze's reading of the *Ethics*, we can feel the tendency to move from the first moment to the second, from speculation to practice, from affirmation to joy. The catalyst that allows Deleuze to make this passage is the Spinozian analysis of power. In the ontological domain, the investigation of the structure of power occupies a privileged position, because the essence of being is its productive causal dynamic. *Causa sui* is the essential pillar that supports being, in that being is defined in its power to exist and produce. All discussions of power, productivity, and causality in Deleuze, as in Spinoza, refer us back to this ontological foundation. The analysis of power, though, is not only an element that brings us back to first principles, it is also the passage that allows the discussion to forge ahead onto new terrain. In the study of Nietzsche, we found that by recognizing the distinction within power between the active and the reactive, we were able to transform the ontological discussion into an ethics. In this study of Spinoza, the same passage through power gains a richer and more extensive function. Here we find an entire system of distinctions within power: between spontaneity and affectivity, between actions and passions, between joy and sadness. This analysis sets the terms for a real conversion within the continuity of the theoretical framework. The investigation of power constitutes the end of speculation and the beginning of practice: It arrives at the hour of midnight, as a Nietzschean transmutation. Power is the crucial link, the point of passage from speculation to practice. The elaboration of this passage will form the pivot of our study. Just as the *Theses on Feuerbach* and *The German Ideology* are said to constitute a "break" in Marx's thought, so too the analysis of power functions as a point of conversion in Spinoza: It is the moment in which we stop striving to think the world, and begin to create it.

Speculation

3.1 Substance and the Real Distinction: Singularity

The opening of the *Ethics* is remarkable. It is precisely these initial passages that have inspired so many readers, in amazement and irritation, in admiration and damnation, to declare that the *Ethics* is an impossible, incomprehensible text—how can one possibly embark on a project starting from the idea of God, from the absolute? This remarkable opening, however, does not appear as problematic to Deleuze. On the contrary, he seems to be perfectly at ease with Spinoza's initial step: Along with Merleau-Ponty, he sees seventeenth-century thought generally as "an innocent way of setting out in one's thinking from the infinite" (*Expressionism in Philosophy: Spinoza* 28, modified). Starting with the infinite is not impossible, but rather quite natural, for Deleuze. We should be careful, though, not to misread this innocence—infinite does not mean indefinite; the infinite substance is not indeterminate. This is the challenge that provides an initial key to Deleuze's analysis and that, according to Deleuze, orients and dominates the first book of the *Ethics*: What kind of distinction is there in the infinite, in the absolutely infinite nature of God? We should note immediately a Bergsonian resonance in this problematic. The connections between Bergsonism and Spinozism are well known, and, although we find no direct references in the text, we can be certain that Deleuze is sensitive to the common features of the two philosophies.[3] However, Deleuze brings the two doctrines together in an unusual and complex way. In effect, Deleuze uses the opening of the *Ethics* as a rereading of Bergson: He presents the proofs of the existence of God and the singularity of substance as an extended meditation on the positive nature of difference and the real foundation of being.

To approach the question of distinctions in Spinoza, of course, we must assume Descartes's position as a point of departure. Deleuze notes the three distinctions of being in Cartesian philosophy: (1) a real distinction between two substances, (2) a modal distinction between a substance and a mode that it implies, and (3) a conceptual distinction (*distinction de raison*) between a substance and an attribute (29). The first error in this system of distinctions, from a Spinozian point of view, is the proposition of number in the definition of substance. By affirming the existence of two substances, Descartes presents the real distinction as a numerical distinction. According to Deleuze, Spinoza challenges this Cartesian idea from two angles in the opening of the *Ethics*: First, he argues that a numerical distinction is never real (*Ethics* IP1-P8), and then that a real distinction is never numerical (P9-P11).[4] In other words, while traditional interpretations have generally identified Spinoza's substance with the number one or with infinity, Deleuze insists that substance is completely removed from the realm of number. Spinoza's first demonstration, that a numerical distinction is never real, rests on the definition of the internal causality of substance (P6C). Number cannot have a substantial nature, because number involves a limitation and thus requires an external cause: "Whatever is of such a nature that there can be many individuals of that nature must . . . have an external cause to exist" (P8S2). From the definition of substance (D3) we know that it cannot involve an external cause. A numerical distinction, then, cannot pertain to substance; or, in other words, a numerical distinction cannot be a real distinction. Starting with P9, however, Spinoza proceeds to the inverse argument, which is really the more fundamental one: Having shown that each attribute corresponds to the same substance (i.e., the numerical distinction is not real), he proceeds to demonstrate that substance envelops all the attributes (i.e., the real distinction is not numerical). This second proof consists of two parts. Spinoza proposes first that the more reality a thing has, the more attributes it must have (P9), and second, he proposes that the more attributes a thing has, the more existence it has (P11S). The two points essentially cover the same ground, and serve together to make the definition of God (D6) a real definition: An absolutely infinite being (God, *ens realissimum*) consists of an absolute infinity of attributes. God is both unique and absolute. It would be absurd to maintain at this point that we are dealing with a numerical domain in which the two endpoints, one and infinity, are united. Spinoza's substance is posed outside of number; the real distinction is not numerical.

Why, though, does this complex logical development of the real distinction appear as fundamental to Deleuze? We should be aware that Spinoza does not use the term "real distinction" when he discusses substance, even though he is certain to be familiar with its usage in Cartesian and Scholastic philosophy. Deleuze introduces this term because it serves to highlight the fundamental relation between being and difference. This strained and tendentious usage of the "real distinction" should draw our attention to Deleuze's original conception of difference. Descartes's real distinction is relational (there is a distinction between x and y); or, more explicitly, it proposes a concept of difference that is entirely founded on negation (x is different from y). Spinoza's challenge is to eliminate the relational, or negative, aspect of the real distinction. Rather than pose the real distinction as a "distinction between" or a "difference from," Spinoza wants to identify the real distinction in itself (there is a distinction in x; or rather, x is different).[5] Once again, we have to be sensitive to the Bergsonian resonances here: "Dissociated from any numerical distinction, real distinction is carried into the absolute. It becomes capable of expressing the difference in being and consequently it brings about the restructuring of other distinctions" (*Expressionism in Philosophy: Spinoza* 39, modified). This statement bears a striking resemblance to a passage in Deleuze's early essay on Bergson: "Thinking internal difference as such, as pure internal difference, arriving at a pure concept of difference, raising difference to the absolute— that is the sense of Bergson's effort" ("La conception de la différence chez Bergson" 90). What we find in common here is the ontological grounding of difference and the central role of difference in the foundation of being. In both Bergson and Spinoza, the essential characteristic of difference is, on one side, its internal causality, and, on the other, its immersion in the absolute. As I have insisted at length, Deleuze's reading of Bergsonian difference depends heavily on a conception of a being that is productive, of an internal and efficient causal dynamic that can be traced back to the materialist tradition and to the Scholastics. This conception takes on its full import in Spinoza: "Spinoza's ontology is dominated by the notions of a *cause of itself, in itself* and *through itself*" (*Expressionism in Philosophy: Spinoza* 162). This internal causal dynamic is what animates the real distinction of being. This is the absolutely positive difference that both supports being in itself and provides the basis for all the differences that characterize real being. To this extent, there is a positive correspondence between Bergson's difference of nature and Spinoza's real distinction: "*Non opposita sed diversa* is the formula of a new logic. Real distinction appeared to open up a new conception of the negative, free from opposition and privation" (*Expressionism in Philosophy: Spinoza* 60). In both cases, a special conception of difference takes the place of opposition: It is a difference that is completely positive, that refers neither to an external cause nor to external mediation—pure difference, difference in itself, difference raised to the absolute.

We should dwell a moment on this point, because its sense is not immediately evident. What can be meant by a distinction that is not numerical? In other words, how can something be different when it is absolutely infinite and indivisible? What is a difference that involves no other? How can we conceive of the absolute without negation? The enormous difficulties posed by these questions point to the ambitious task of the opening of the *Ethics*: "Spinoza needed all the resources of an original conceptual frame to bring out the power and the actuality of positive infinity" (*Expressionism in Philosophy: Spinoza* 28). Here we are confronted with the Spinozian principle of the singularity of being. As a first approximation, we could say that singularity is the union of monism with the absolute positivity of pantheism: The unique substance directly infuses and animates the entire world. The problem with this definition is that it leaves open an idealistic interpretation of substance, and allows for a confusion between the infinite and the indefinite. In other words, from an idealist perspective, absolute substance might be read as an indetermination, and pantheism might be read as acosmism. Deleuze's reading, however, closes off this possibility. Being is singular not only in that it is unique and absolutely infinite, but, more important, in that it is *remarkable*. This is the impossible opening of the *Ethics*. Singular being as substance is not "distinct from" or "different from" any thing outside itself; if it were, we would have to conceive it partly through another thing, and thus it would not be substance. And yet, being is not indifferent. Here we can begin to appreciate the radicality of Spinoza's definition of substance: "By substance I understand what is in itself and is conceived through itself, i.e., that whose concept does not require the concept of another thing, from which it must be formed" (D3). The distinction of being rises from within. *Causa sui* means that being is both infinite and definite: Being is remarkable. The first task of the real distinction, then, is to define being as singular, to recognize its difference without reference to, or dependence on, any other thing. The real nonnumerical distinction defines the singularity of being, in that being is absolutely infinite and indivisible at the same time that it is distinct and determinate. Singularity, in Deleuze, has nothing to do with individuality or particularity. It is, rather, the correlate of efficient causality and internal difference: The singular is remarkable because it is different in itself.

3.2 Expressive Attributes and the Formal Distinction: Univocity

At this point, it seems that we can identify Deleuze's reading of Bergsonian virtuality with that of Spinozian substance in that both propose singular conceptions of being animated by an absolutely positive and internal difference.[6] Once we propose this common terrain of the singularity of being, however, Spinoza's conception of the attributes rises up as a real departure and as a profound contribution. We have established thus far that the real distinction is not a numerical distinction, or, in Bergsonian terms, that a difference of nature is not a difference of degree; now, with Spinoza's theory of the attributes, Deleuze will extend this argument beyond Bergson to show that the real distinction is also a formal distinction. Through the investigation of the formal distinction of the attributes, Deleuze arrives at a second Spinozian principle of ontology: the principle of the univocity of being. In order to grasp the univocity of being, we have to begin with an investigation of its vocality, its expressivity. The Spinozian attributes, on Deleuze's reading, are the expressions of being. Traditionally, the problem of the attributes of God is closely tied to that of divine names. Spinoza transforms this tradition by giving the attribute the active role in divine expression: "The attribute is no longer attributed, but is in some sense 'attributive.' Each attribute expresses an essence, and attributes it to substance" (45). The issue of divine names becomes a problematic of divine expression.

Deleuze sets up a simple progression of theological paradigms to situate Spinoza's theory of expressive attributes. Negative theologies in general affirm that God is the cause of the world, but deny that the essence of the world is the essence of God. In other words, although the world is a divine expression, the divine essence always surpasses or transcends the essence of its expression: "What conceals also expresses, but what expresses still conceals" (53). Thus, God as essence or substance can only be defined negatively, as an eminent, transcendent, and concealed source of expression. The God of negative theology is expressive, but with a certain essential reserve. Positive theologies, on the contrary, affirm God as both cause and essence of the world. However, among these theories there are important distinctions in the way that they affirm God's positivity. Deleuze finds it most important to distinguish expressive theologies from analogical theologies. In the Thomistic tradition, for example, the qualities attributed to God imply an analogical relation between God and the creatures of the world. This conception both elevates God to an eminent position and renders the expression of being equivocal. God and the creatures are different in form, and thus cannot be said in the same sense, but analogy is employed precisely to bridge this gap. Analogy proposes to reconcile the essential identity and the formal difference between God and things. Spinoza's theory of the attribute reverses this formula: "Attributes are forms common to God, whose essence they constitute, and to modes or creatures which imply them essentially" (47). Spinoza's attribute, in contrast to theories of analogy, proposes a commonality of form and a distinction of essences: "Spinoza's method is neither abstract nor analogical. It is a formal method based on community" (48). This Spinozian distinction of essence, though, should not be referred back to a negative theological conception. Through the attributes (the expressions), substance (the expressing agent) is absolutely immanent in the world of modes (the expressed). The distinction between the essence of the expressing agent and the essence of the expressed does not deny the immanence of the one in the other. The divine is absolutely expressed; nothing is hidden; there is neither reserve nor excess. Spinoza's conception of the singularity of being shows clearly his opposition to this negative theological paradigm: Immanence is opposed to eminence; pantheism is opposed to transcendence. Spinoza's God is fully expressed in the world, without reserve. Spinozian monism opposes all dualism, both negative and analogical. The central element that allows for this absolute expression is the commonality of forms contained in the attribute.

The distinction between expression and analogy becomes clearer when Deleuze distinguishes attributes from properties. "Properties are not properly speaking attributes, precisely because they are not *expressive*" (50). The properties of God (omnipotence, omniscience, perfection, etc.) do not express anything of the nature of God: Properties are mute. They appear to us as signs, as revelations, as commandments. Properties are notions impressed on us that cannot make us understand anything about nature, because they do not present us with a common form. Deleuze distinguishes, therefore, between two senses of "the word of God": one that refers to the attribute as expression, and another that refers to the property as sign: "*A sign always attaches to a property*; it always signifies a commandment; and it grounds our obedience. *Expression always relates to an attribute*; it expresses an essence, that is, a nature in the infinitive; it makes it known to us" (57). Once again, the expression of the attributes can only take place through the common forms of being. This conception can be seen from two sides: On one hand, by means of the attributes, God is absolutely *immanent* (fully expressed) in the world of the modes; and on the other hand, through the common forms of the attributes, the modes *participate* fully in divine substance. Immanence and participation are the two sides of the expression of the attributes. It is this participation that distinguishes between the understanding given by the expressive attributes and the obedience imposed by the analogous properties. A system of signs tells us nothing about being; the mute signs and the commandments of semiology close off ontology. Only expression can open up our knowledge of being.[7]

Thus far, we have critiqued negative theology and analogical positive theology on the basis of the expression of the attributes through the common forms of being. To an extent, the conception of common forms is implied by the real distinction: The singularity of being requires the absolute immanence of the divine in the world, because if God were not absolutely immanent, we would need to distinguish between two substances. Absolute immanence, however, is a necessary, but not sufficient, condition for univocity. The attributes are not only characterized by an internal common form (that follows from immanence), but also by an external plurality. In other words, in order to pursue this theory of an expressive positive theology, the formal commonality embodied in each infinite attribute has to be complemented by the formal distinction among the different attributes. The divine essence is not only expressed in one attribute, but in an infinite number of *formally distinct* attributes. To fill out this positive theological framework, then, Deleuze traces Spinoza's theory of the attributes back to Duns Scotus:[8] "It was without doubt Scotus who pursued farther than any other the enterprise of a positive theology. He denounces at once the negative eminence of the Neoplatonists and the pseudoaffirmation of the Thomists" (63). The positive theology of Duns Scotus is characterized by the theory of the formal distinction. This concept provides a logical mechanism whereby he can maintain both the differences among the attributes and the commonality within each attribute: The attributes are formally distinct and ontologically identical. "There are here as it were two orders, that of formal reason and that of being, with the plurality in one perfectly according with the simplicity of the other" (64). The positive expression of the formally distinct attributes constitutes, for Spinoza as for Duns Scotus, a conception of the univocity of being. *Univocity means precisely that being is expressed always and everywhere in the same voice*; in other words, the attributes each express being in a different form but in the same sense. Therefore, univocity implies a formal difference between attributes, but a real and absolute ontological commonality among the attributes.

Deleuze is careful to point out, however, that Spinoza's theory of univocal being well surpasses that of Duns Scotus, thanks to the Spinozian conception of the expressivity of the attributes. In Duns Scotus, what are called attributes—justice, goodness, wisdom, and so on—are really merely properties. In the final analysis, Duns Scotus remains too much of a theologian, and thus he cannot abandon a certain eminence of the divine: "For his theological, that is to say 'creationist,' perspective forced him to conceive univocal Being as a *neutralized, indifferent* concept" (67). In Duns Scotus, God the creator is not the cause of all things *in the same sense* that it is the cause of itself. Since univocal being in Duns Scotus is not absolutely singular, it remains somewhat indifferent, somewhat inexpressive. Spinoza's real distinction, though, elevates univocity to the level of affirmation. In the Spinozian attribute, the expression of being is the affirmation of being: "Attributes are affirmations; but affirmation, in its essence is always formal, actual, univocal: therein lies its expressivity. Spinoza's philosophy is a philosophy of pure affirmation. Affirmation is the speculative principle on which hangs the whole of the *Ethics*" (60). In the Spinozian context, Deleuze gives affirmation an original and precise definition: It is a speculative principle based on the absolute singularity and univocity of being, or, in other words, on the full expressivity of being. And here, once again, we can recognize a typical Bergsonian appreciation of Spinoza: "Spinoza allows us to put a finger on what is heroic in speculation" (*Ecrits et paroles* 587). Affirmation constitutes the pinnacle, the heroic moment of a pure, speculative philosophy.

Remark: Ontological Speculation

Let us pause for a moment and consider carefully the ground we have covered. In effect, Deleuze has read the first two great steps of the Spinozian system, the elaborations of substance and the attributes, as an alternative logic of speculation—not in opposition to, but completely autonomous from, the Hegelian progression. This conceptual autonomy demonstrates not only how Spinoza represents a turning point in the evolution of Deleuze's work, but also how Deleuze's interpretation constitutes a revolution for Spinoza studies, which had been long dominated in Continental philosophy by a Hegelian reading. In reading Deleuze's study of Nietzsche, we argued that Deleuze was disengaging his own thought from the dialectical terrain through the theory of the total critique. In Spinoza, this process is complete. However, even though there is no mention of Hegel in the entire text, we can easily construct a comparison with Hegelian ontology in order to demonstrate the important conceptual autonomy marked by Deleuze's Spinozian foundation. Hegel's own interpretation and critique of Spinozian ontology, in fact, serve to highlight the differences of Deleuze's work; from a Hegelian perspective, we will be able to recognize the radical departure constituted by Deleuze's reading of the singularity of substance and the univocity of the attributes in Spinoza.

The crux of the issue here is the Hegelian conception of determination. Hegel claims not only that Spinozian substance is indeterminate, but that all determinations are dissolved in the absolute (*Science of Logic* 536). According to Hegel, the unique and absolute being of Spinozism cannot provide a basis for determination or difference because it involves no other or limitation. Determinate being must negate and subsume its other within itself in order to attain quality and reality. The Spinozian conception of singularity is a logical impossibility. The definition of being as singular is precisely what irritates Hegel most, and it is the point that he refuses to recognize: Spinozism, he claims, is an acosmism. Singularity is, in fact, a real threat to Hegel because it constitutes the refusal of the speculative foundation of dialectics. In this context we can understand clearly the theoretical demands that could drive Hegel to give this final judgement of Spinoza: "The cause of his death was consumption, from which he had long been a sufferer; this was in harmony with his system of philosophy, according to which all particularity and individuality pass away in the one substance" (*Lectures on the History of Philosophy* 257). When determination is denied, so too Spinoza the philosopher dissolves into nothingness.

Deleuze's reading of the real distinction stands in sharp contrast (but not opposition!) to this interpretation. As we have argued, the real distinction presents being as different in itself. Singular being is not different from anything outside being, and neither is it indifferent or abstract: It is simply remarkable. It would be false, then, to set up an opposition between singular being and determinate being. Singularity is and is not determination. In other words, Spinoza's being, the unique substance, is determinate in the sense that it is qualified, that it is different. However, it is not determinate in the sense of being limited. This is where Deleuze's discussion of number comes into play. If substance were to be limited (or to have number) it would have to involve an external cause. Substance, on the contrary, is absolutely infinite, it is cause of itself. *Causa sui* cannot be read in any ideal sense: Being is the material and efficient cause of itself, and this continual act of self-production brings with it all the real determinations of the world. "Omnis determinatio est negatio"? Clearly, there is no

room for this equation in Deleuze's Spinoza—not even as a point of opposition. Being is never indeterminate; it brings with it immediately all the
freshness and materiality of reality. I would argue that here, with this real
conceptual autonomy from the Hegelian problematic, we can recognize a
significant evolution of Deleuze's thought. In the earlier Bergson studies,
we noted a certain equivocation on this issue. There was a tendency for
Deleuze, along with Bergson, to oppose determination, and to affirm indetermination instead. The proposition of indetermination allowed that
being would not be restricted or constrained by an external cause. Both
aspects of this position, the opposition to determination and the acceptance of indetermination, have proved to be problematic. In effect, in opposing the rhythm of the dialectical process of determination, Deleuze was
accepting its opposite (indetermination), and thus remained locked on the
dialectical terrain. However, in the Spinozian context, we find that determination and indetermination are equally inadequate terms. Singularity is
the concept that marks the internal difference, the real distinction that
qualifies absolutely infinite being as real without recourse to a dialectic of
negations. The concept of singularity constitutes the real dislocation from
the Hegelian theoretical horizon.

This difference in the two interpretations of the Spinozian substance
continues and develops in the interpretations of the attributes. To a great
extent, Hegel's reading of the attribute follows directly from his interpretation of substance: Since substance is an infinite indetermination, the attribute serves to limit substance, to determine it (*Science of Logic* 537).
Hegel conceives of the theoretical movement from substance to the attributes as the shadow image of the dialectic of determination, which is
doomed to failure because it omits the fundamental play of negations.
Deleuze's reading of the attribute moves in a very different direction, again
based on his different interpretation of substance. Since, in his view, substance is already real and qualified, there is no question of determination,
but rather, according to Deleuze, the attributes fill the role of expression.
Through the attributes we recognize the absolute immanence or expressivity of being. Furthermore, the infinite and equal expressions constitute
the univocity of being, in that it is always and everywhere expressed in the
same voice.

If the central issue in the interpretation of substance is determination,
the interpretation of the attributes focuses on emanation. Deleuze's theory
of expression effectively constitutes a challenge to Hegel's judgment that
Spinozism is an "oriental conception of *emanation*" (*Science of Logic*
538). According to Hegel, the Spinozian movement of being is an irrecu-
perative series of degradations: "The process of emanation is taken only as
a *happening*, the becoming only as a progressive loss" (539). Deleuze of-

fers us a response to this Hegelian critique in the form of an extended analysis of the relation between emanation and immanence in the history of philosophy. As one might expect, this Deleuzian history of philosophy completely disregards the Hegelian and dialectical tradition, by considering only positive ontological processes. This positive movement is precisely what philosophies of emanation and immanence share: Both are animated by an internal causality. "Their common characteristic is that neither leaves itself: they produce *while remaining in themselves*" (*Expressionism in Philosophy: Spinoza* 171). Since being is singular, its production can involve no other. Nonetheless, there is an important difference in the way in which the emanative cause and the immanent cause produce. "A cause is immanent . . . when its effect is 'immanate' [immané] in the cause, rather than emanating from it. What defines an immanent cause is that its effect is in it—in it, of course, as in something else, but still being and remaining in it" (172). The difference between the essence of the immanent cause and the essence of its effect, therefore, can never be interpreted as a degradation: At the level of essences, there is an absolute ontological equality between cause and effect. In an emanative process, on the other hand, the externality of the effect with respect to the cause allows for a successive degradation in the causal chain and an inequality of essences.

We can clearly see at this point that Spinoza's ontology is a philosophy of immanence, not emanation. The essential equality of immanence demands a univocal being: "Not only is being equal in itself, but it appears equally present in all beings" (173). Immanence denies any form of eminence or hierarchy in being: The principle of the univocity of the attributes requires that being be expressed equally in all of its forms. Therefore, univocal expression is incompatible with emanation. What Deleuze's explanation makes clear is that Spinoza's ontology, a combination of immanence and expression, is not susceptible to the Hegelian critique of the dispersion, the "progressive loss" of being. Deleuze explains this with the terms of medieval philosophy, citing Nicholas of Cusa: "God is the universal complication, in the sense that everything is in it; and the universal explication, in the sense that it is in everything" (175). The immanence and expression of Spinozism, according to Deleuze, presents a modern version of this medieval couple, *complicare-explicare*. Inasmuch as expression is an explicative or centrifugal movement, it is also a complicative or centripetal movement, gathering being back within itself. Deleuze's analysis, then, not only presents Spinoza as an alternative logic of ontological speculation, but also provides us with the terms to respond to the Hegelian critique of Spinoza.

We have thus far treated Deleuze's reading of the opening of the *Ethics* (roughly as far as IP14), which presents in compact form the principles of ontological speculation. We should be very clear about the simplicity of what has been developed thus far: "a logical constitution of substance, a 'composition' in which there is nothing physical" (79). This logical constitution developed in the opening of the *Ethics* consists of two principles: singularity and univocity. We can affirm this same claim in another way by saying that in the opening of the *Ethics*, Spinoza shows that the definition of God (D6) is not merely a nominal definition, but a real definition: "This is the only definition that presents us with a nature, the expressive nature of the absolute" (81). Through the expression of the absolute as singular and univocal, Spinoza accomplishes a logical constitution of the idea of God. If we read this theological terminology in a traditional sense, though, we will certainly be disappointed. Bergson, for one, reacts to the purely logical character of Spinoza's presentation: "The God of the first part of the *Ethics* is engendered outside of all experience, as a circle would be for a geometrician who has never seen one" (quoted in Mossé-Bastide, "Bergson et Spinoza" 71, from Bergson's course at the Collège de France, 1912). Spinoza is not, however, constructing an image or idea of God in any conventional sense. He is excavating being in order to discover the real ontological principles of speculation. What Spinoza has arrived at is simply the fundamental genetic principles, singularity and univocity, that guide the production and constitution of being. There is nothing hypothetical about the opening of the *Ethics*, then; instead, it is a speculative development of the genetic sequence of being, "a genealogy of substance" (Deleuze, "Spinoza et la méthode générale de M. Gueroult" 432). The principles that demonstrate the reality of the definition of God (D6) are those of the life of substance itself; they are the a priori constitution of being (*Expressionism in Philosophy: Spinoza* 81). When Deleuze says that this definition is a genetic definition, he means precisely that the principles of being are active and constructive: From these principles being itself unfolds.

   This is all we know about being (about God) at this point in the analysis: It is singular and it is univocal. There is an implicit polemic in this affirmation about the nature and the limits of speculation. The truths that we can learn through speculation are very few and very simple. Speculation does not constitute the world or construct being; it merely can provide us with the fundamental principles by which being is constituted. Spinoza is clearly conscious of this fact, and if we demand more of his speculation we are bound to be disappointed, as Bergson is, with his "God made of ice." Spinoza's real constitution of being takes place in another field of activity, in an ontological practice, which is autonomous from the field of speculation. On this point, we can see clearly why Spinozian thought is not recuperable within a Hegelian (or within any idealist) framework. Ontological speculation is not productive; it is not constitutive of being. Speculation merely traces the contours of being's productive dynamic. Soon we will turn our attention to the constitutive nature of Spinozian practice, but first we should investigate a third and final ontological principle: the principle of the powers of being, without which Spinoza's thought would remain speculative and never make the conversion to a practical philosophy.

3.3 The Powers of Being

The seeds of the Spinozian principle of power can be found in the a posteriori proofs of the existence of God. Deleuze prepares his treatment of these proofs by first presenting the Cartesian a priori proof as a framework. Descartes's proof is based on the quantities of perfection or reality: A cause must have at least as much reality as its effect; the cause of an idea must have at least as much formal reality as the idea has objective reality; now I have the idea of an infinitely perfect being; and so on. Deleuze claims that Spinoza takes up this Cartesian proof in his *Short Treatise* with an original modification. Like Descartes, Spinoza begins from the idea of God and asserts that the cause of this idea must exist and contain formally all that the idea contains objectively (*Short Treatise* I:3). However, the Cartesian axiom about the quantities of perfection or reality is not sufficient to support this proof. In its place, Spinoza substitutes an axiom of power that links the power to think with the power to exist or act: "The intellect has no more power to know than its objects have to exist and act; the power to think and know cannot be greater than a necessarily correlative power of existing" (*Expressionism in Philosophy: Spinoza* 86, modified). Deleuze presents this a priori proof of the *Short Treatise*, however, as merely a midpoint in Spinoza's development.

The axiom of power attains a mature deployment in the a posteriori proofs in the *Ethics*. Spinoza offers three demonstrations of the proposition that God necessarily exists, but Deleuze is primarily interested in the third because in this proof Spinoza no longer passes through the idea of God and the power to think, but begins directly with the power to exist. Spinoza's argument proceeds as follows: (1) To be able to exist is to have power; (2) it would be absurd to say that finite beings exist while an absolutely infinite being does not exist, because that would be to say that the finite beings are more powerful; (3) therefore, either nothing exists or an absolutely infinite being also exists; (4) since we exist, an absolutely infinite being necessarily exists (IP11D3). The importance of this proof for our purposes is not its logical coherence, but rather its use of "the power to exist" in the logical foundation. Spinoza makes power a principle of being.

Power is the essence of being that presents essence in existence. The intimate nexus in Spinoza that unites cause, power, production, and essence is the dynamic core that makes his speculative system into a dynamic project. "The identity of power and essence means: power is always act or, at least, in action [*en acte*]" (93). God produces as it exists. Many commentators have recognized in Spinoza's conception of power a naturalism that is in direct opposition to Descartes, and that draws on the work of Renaissance thinkers such as Giordano Bruno. Ferdinand Alquié, for example, explains that this Spinozian nexus constitutes an active principle: "Spinoza's nature (is) above all spontaneity, an active principle of development" (*Nature et vérité* 9).[9] Deleuze accepts this conception of Spinoza's naturalism, but for him it presents only half the picture. In effect, Deleuze complements the reference to Renaissance naturalism with a second reference, a reference to modern materialism (Hobbes, in particular). Spinoza's conception of power is not only a principle of action, Deleuze claims, but also, to the same extent, a principle of affection. In other words, the essence of nature as power implies equally a production and a sensibility: "All power bears with it a corresponding and inseparable power to be affected" (93). Power in Spinoza has two sides that are always equal and indivisible: the power to effect and the power to be affected, production and sensibility. Therefore, Spinoza can add a second aspect to the affirmation of the a posteriori proof of God: Not only does God have an absolutely infinite power to exist, God also has the power to be affected in an absolutely infinite number of ways.

This is precisely the point at which, in *Nietzsche and Philosophy*, Deleuze identified a link between Spinoza and Nietzsche (62). A will to power is always accompanied by a feeling of power. Furthermore, this Nietzschean pathos does not involve a body "suffering" from passions; rather, pathos plays an active, productive role. The Spinozian couple power-affectivity echoes some of these Nietzschean elements. Our use of the term "sensibility" to try to describe the power to be affected may well be misleading. An affection in Spinozian terminology may be an action or a passion, depending on whether the affection results from an internal or an external cause. Therefore, the power to exist of a mode always corresponds to a power to be affected, and this power to be affected "is always filled, either by affections produced by external things (called passive affections), or by affections explained by the mode's own essence (called active affections)" (*Expressionism in Philosophy: Spinoza* 93, modified). The plenitude of being, in Spinoza as in Nietzsche, means not only that being is always and everywhere fully expressed, without any transcendental and ineffable reserve, but also that the power to be affected, which corresponds to the power to exist, is completely filled with active and passive affections.

These two distinctions constitute our initial essay in discerning the internal structure of power.

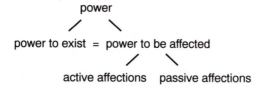

We can begin to see at this point how Spinoza's proposition of the equivalence between the power to exist and the power to be affected can lead us toward a practical theory. To understand the nature of power we have to discover the internal structures of power; but when we investigate the first side of the equation, the power to exist, power appears as pure spontaneity. Its structure is opaque to us, and our analysis is blocked. However, once Spinoza has proposed the equivalence between the power to exist and the power to be affected, we can shift our investigation to the other side of the equation. Here we find a truly differentiated structure and a rich terrain for our analysis. When we pose the question of cause in this context, we find a real distinction: Our power to be affected is constituted by active affections (internally caused) and passive affections (externally caused). Immediately, this distinction suggests the outlines of an ethical, and ultimately practical, project: How can we favor active affections so that our power to be affected will be filled to a greater extent with active rather than passive affections? At this point, however, we are unable to address this task, because we still know too little about the structure of power.

Nonetheless, we should note that Spinoza's principle of power always presents itself as a principle of conversion—a conversion from speculation to practice, from the analysis of being to the constitution of being. Spinoza's power enters the scene at the hour of midnight, at the moment of Nietzsche's transmutation. This conversion is possible because Spinoza's analysis of the internal structure of power, pressing the question of the causal dynamic at every point, illuminates the real steps that we can take in constituting ourselves and our world through practice. We must be patient, though, and not jump too far ahead. With Spinoza's proposition of the principle of power, we have only opened the door (or as Althusser might say, "nous avons ouvert des voies") toward the development of an ontological practice. At present, there is more work to be done in order to prepare this terrain; we must turn back to the three ontological principles we have identified—singularity, univocity, and power—and develop them into a full speculative logic of being.

Ontological Expression

3.4 The Interpretation of the Attributes:
Problems of a Materialist Ontology

As we have seen, the Spinozian theory of the attribute solves many problems; but it also raises many others. One of the most serious difficulties
that it poses is the threat of an idealist or subjectivist tendency in Spinoza's
thought. What is most important to Deleuze in this regard is to maintain a
strictly materialist interpretation of Spinoza's ontology (and we will see
that there are several tensions involved with maintaining this position).
This discussion will help us flesh out the role that materialism plays in
Deleuze's thought.

Materialism should never be confused with a simple priority of body
over mind, of the physical over the intellectual. Rather, materialism repeatedly appears in the history of philosophy as a corrective to idealism, as a
denial of the priority of mind over body. Spinoza corrects Descartes just as
Marx corrects Hegel. This materialist correction is not an inversion of the
priority, but the proposition of an equality in principle between the corporeal and the intellectual. Deleuze makes clear that this refusal of the priority of the intellect serves to point toward and reinforce the priority of being
equally over all of its attributes (thought, extension, etc.). From this perspective, the only true ontology must be materialist. Any privilege of the
intellect, in other words, would subvert the ontological structure of the
system, so that not only matter but also being itself would somehow be
dependent on thought. Deleuze finds it necessary, then, to combat an idealist account of being not only in order to valorize the material world, but
more important to preserve the coherence of the ontological perspective.
The intellectual and the corporeal are equal expressions of being: This is
the fundamental principle of a materialist ontology.

In the context of the Spinozian system, we can identify the central issue
in the very definition of the attribute: "By attribute I understand *what the
intellect perceives of a substance*, as constituting its essence" (*Ethics* ID4,
my emphasis). One of the problems that presents itself immediately is that
the definition grants a certain priority to the attribute of thought over the
other attributes: Thought is the means of perceiving all the attributes of
substance, including thought itself. Several examples illustrating the role
of the attribute, such as those in Letter 9 to Simon de Vries, give an even
more problematic explanation. In this letter, Spinoza offers two examples
of how in the attributes "one and the same thing can be designated by two
names." The first of these two is perhaps the more problematic: "I say that
by Israel I understand the third patriarch; I understand the same by Jacob,

the name that was given him because he had seized his brother's heel."
The distinction here is merely nominal and, more important, the difference resides not in the object perceived but in the perceiving subject, not
directly in being but in the intellect.

In Spinoza studies there is a long-standing controversy over the interpretation of the attributes.[10] The nucleus of the dispute involves the position of the attribute with respect to substance on one side, and with respect
to the intellect on the other: It is a question of the priority of *ratio essendi*
and *ratio cognoscendi*. The idealist or subjectivist interpretation defines
the attribute primarily as a form of knowledge, and not as a form of being.
Hegel's presentation in the *Science of Logic* is the seminal reading in this
tradition.[11] As we noted earlier, Hegel conceives of the attribute as the determination or limitation of substance that is dependent on the intellect
and that "proceeds outside the absolute" (538), that is, "which appears as
external and immediate over against substance" (537). Martial Gueroult
points out that there is a logical contradiction in this reading that weakens
the foundations of Spinozian ontology: The attributes cannot be dependent on the intellect because the intellect is a mode of thought, and therefore ontologically posterior to the attributes. "In fact, if the attributes were
to result from the idea that the intellect had of substance, the intellect
would be anterior to them, and consequently anterior to the attribute of
which it is a mode, which is absurd" (I, 50). Hegel himself recognizes this
contradiction, but seems to credit it to an error in the Spinozian system
rather than to a fault of his interpretation (*Science of Logic* 537). However,
the primary issue at stake here, I would maintain, is not the logical contradiction of the subjectivist reading, but rather the priority that it grants to
the intellect. The question, I repeat, is the relative import of the *ratio essendi* and the *ratio cognoscendi* in the system as a whole. What is at stake,
in other words, are the very terms of a materialist ontology, an ontology
that does not found being in thought.

Deleuze provides us with an alternative reading of the Spinozian
attributes—an objectivist, ontological interpretation. According to
Deleuze, when Spinoza presents the attribute as merely a way of knowing
or conceiving, as in Letter 9, he is giving only a partial or simplified explanation of the attribute's real role (61). The attribute does not depend on
the intellect; on the contrary, the intellect plays only a secondary role in the
functioning of the attributes, as an objective and invisible agent of representation. "All formally distinct attributes are referred by the intellect to an
ontologically single substance. But the intellect only reproduces objectively the nature of the forms it apprehends" (65). In other words, the relation of the attributes to substance is prior to and independent of the intellect's apprehension of this relation; the intellect merely reproduces in

objective or cognitive terms the primary ontological relation. The *ratio essendi* is prior to the *ratio cognoscendi*. This objectivist interpretation succeeds in preserving the ontological integrity of the system, and it resolves the contradiction posed by granting a foundational role to the intellect in the theory of the attributes. Nonetheless, we must recognize that we cannot maintain this thesis without a certain strain. Let us return, for example, to the definition of the attributes: "By attribute I understand *what the intellect perceives of a substance*, as constituting its essence" (*Ethics* ID4, my emphasis). How can the objectivist interpretation account for this "quod intellectus de substantiâ percipit" without giving a foundational role to the intellect? (And we should note that reference to the original Latin offers us no way out in this dilemma.) Furthermore, even if we are to accept the intellect as secondary in the foundation of the attribute, how are we to understand what Deleuze describes as its "objective reproduction" of the nature of the forms it apprehends? This "reproduction" is certainly a very weak conception of expression.

Deleuze does not seem to be disturbed by these problems (or perhaps he is determined not to be sidetracked by them), and he does not treat this issue in any depth. What is clear, however, is the insistence of Deleuze's effort to preserve the ontological integrity of the system and combat any priority of thought over the other attributes, even when this effort seems to go against clear statements in the text. The stakes here go well beyond the realm of Spinoza studies, and refer instead to the nature of the return to ontology central to Deleuze's philosophy and the radical difference it marks with respect to other contemporary philosophical positions. Deleuze's philosophy has to be recognized in its difference from both the idealist ontological tradition and any deontological approach to philosophy; instead, through the interpretation of the attributes Deleuze is working out the dimensions of a materialist ontology.

Remark: Speculative Production and Theoretical Practice

When we broaden our perspective beyond the specific questions of Spinoza interpretation, we can see that Deleuze's objectivist reading marks him as radically out of sync with the intellectual movements of his time, as sustaining a precariously minoritarian theoretical position. The intellectual hegemony in 1960s France of the "masters of suspicion," the partisans of the trilogy Marx-Nietzsche-Freud,[12] although to a certain extent anti-Hegelian, nonetheless (if we can allow ourselves a transposition to the terrain of the Spinozian controversy) have to be counted on the side of a subjectivist reading of the attributes. The various *mots d'ordre* that sprang up from different camps throughout the French intellectual scene in this period all insist on the foundational role of the intellect, of the *ratio cognoscendi*; consider, for example, the importance of the widespread discourse on "vision," on the seen and the non-seen, or rather the focus on "interpretation" as a privileged field of investigation. Deleuze's proposition of an objectivist ontological speculation in Spinoza runs counter to this entire stream of thought. The general trend, in fact, seems to constitute a forceful attack on Deleuze's position.

So as not to fall into abstract generalization, let us briefly investigate Althusser's reading of Marx as an example—perhaps not a representative example, but certainly one that was influential. One element that Althusser wants to bring into focus, and to bring into question, is the act of reading itself: reading Marx's *Capital*, reading the classical economists, reading capitalist society. Althusser wants us to find in Marx a revolution in the theory of knowledge: "We must completely reorganize the idea we have of knowledge, we must abandon the specular myths of immediate vision and reading, and conceive knowledge as a production" (*Reading Capital* 24). We can distinguish two elements in Althusser's effort to conceive of knowledge as a production. First, we must grasp that there is a distinction between the object of knowledge and the real object—or, to follow Althusser in a Spinozian example, there is a distinction between the idea of a circle and a really existing circle (40ff.). As a second step, however, we must recognize that the importance of this distinction lies in the fact that the two domains exist under different conditions: While the real object is given, the thought object is produced in a specific relation to reality. "No doubt there is a relation between *thought*-about-the-real and this *real*, but it is a relation of knowledge" (87). Althusser's insistence on the centrality of *ratio cognoscendi* is a characteristic central to phenomenological speculation. Before we can consider real things in themselves, according to phenomenologists, we must consider how these things are presented to our consciousness, to our intellect. This is where the Spinozian attribute reappears at the heart of the discussion: "quod intellectus de substantiâ percipit." Althusser's strategy of reading, along with phenomenological speculation in general, coincides perfectly with a subjectivist interpretation of the attribute. Subjectivist reading puts an end to the myth of pure speculation, of a "specular" speculation: There is no innocent or objective reading of the world, of society, of political economy.

At first sight, Althusser's critique, which in this respect is representative of a general intellectual movement, seems to fall directly and heavily on Deleuze's objectivist reading of the attributes. Deleuze gives the intellect precisely the "specular" role that Althusser denounces: "The intellect only *reproduces objectively* the nature of the forms it apprehends" (*Expressionism in Philosophy: Spinoza* 65). How can Deleuze possibly maintain the theory of a specular, objective intellect? How, when the entire French philosophical community is focusing on the *productive* nature of knowledge, can Deleuze relegate the apprehension of the intellect to a *reproductive* role? We are certainly faced with conflicting positions here. Deleuze's philosophy is not a phenomenology. However, when we examine the matter closely, we find that in certain respects the Althusserian critique does not, in fact, directly address Deleuze's argument. First of all, Deleuze is not ignoring the centrality of production; rather, he gives the functioning of the intellect a reproductive role in the theory of the attribute, because the primary production is elsewhere. We have emphasized throughout our reading of Deleuze's various works that his ontology is founded on the conception that being is a productive dynamic. In the Bergson study, we related this conception to the causal discourse of the Scholastics, and in Spinoza we can trace it to Renaissance naturalism. We could summarize Deleuze's ontology in precisely these terms: Being is productive in direct, immediate, and absolutely positive terms. Every discussion of causality and difference is based on this foundation. With this in mind, we can interpret Deleuze's position on the *reproductive* role of the intellect as principally an affirmation of the *productive* role of being. Thus, we can hazard a preliminary Deleuzian response to our first Althusserian critique: Bringing cognitive production to center stage in philosophy masks the fundamental productive dynamic of being that is really antecedent to the intellect, in logical and ontological terms.

This first response, however, can only serve partially to deflect the critique, not answer it. We can approach a more adequate explanation of Deleuze's position if we bring into question the *domain* proper to speculation. Deleuze's speculation does claim an objective representation, but it applies merely to a very specific terrain. Society, capital, and its economy are not appropriate objects of speculation; rather, in Deleuze, speculation is brought to bear exclusively on ontological issues, and, as we have insisted, it arrives at very few, and very simple, ontological principles. Against a phenomenological speculation, Deleuze poses a purely ontological speculation. What would it mean to conceive of this ontological speculation as production? We would have to say, in line with a subjectivist ontology, that singularity, univocity, and power are not principles of being (as real objects), but rather products of our intellectual activity (as objects of our knowledge). In other words, we would have to say that they are not actually principles of being, but rather "quod intellectus de substantiâ percipit." This subjectivization of being would undermine the ontological foundation of the Spinozian system in its entirety. The objectivist interpretation of the attributes claims simply that there are certain principles of being that are prior to, and independent of, the productive power of thought;

these principles constitute the field of speculation. Deleuze, then, tries to preserve the specificity of ontology within its specific domain. What lies outside of the realm of ontological speculation is treated by Deleuze in empirical terms—it will be the foundation of Deleuze's conception of practice.

This second Deleuzian response, however, is still open to a further Althusserian critique. The recognition of the production involved in knowledge and its distinction from reality, according to Althusser, is the defining factor of all materialism: "If we do not respect it, we inevitably fall into either speculative idealism or empiricist idealism" (*Reading Capital* 87). Althusser's materialist and phenomenological speculation is precisely what allows him to propose his famous concept of practice within theory, "the theory of theoretical practice." The objectivist interpretation of the attributes, on the contrary, banishes practice from the field of speculation. Deleuze's thought, then, appears as idealism on both sides of this practico-theoretical synthesis: a speculative idealism and an empirical idealism held loosely together in one philosophy. Clearly, Deleuze's conception of practice does not escape Althusser's indictment: "It is enough to pronounce the word *practice*, which, understood in an ideological (empiricist or idealist) way, is only the mirror image, the counter-connotation of *theory* (the pair of 'contraries' practice and theory composing the two terms of a specular field), to reveal the play on words that is its seat" (57-58). From this perspective, Deleuze's practice, which pretends to be autonomous from speculation, is merely the compliant specular counterpart to objectivist and idealist speculation in a fraudulent word game. Drawing on one of Althusser's favorite texts, the *Theses on Feuerbach*, we have to level the accusation that Deleuze's philosophy can have no practical power; it can merely attempt to think the world, not change it.

With the critique of practice, we have touched the heart of the matter, but we do not yet have control of the terms to investigate it further. Althusser's challenge can serve, for the present, as a critical axis to orient our discussion and highlight the difference marked by Deleuze's approach. Pure ontology and absolute materialism: These are the complementary positions that Deleuze sustains against the tide of his contemporaries.

3.5 Combatting the Privileges of Thought

We must return now to consider in greater depth Deleuze's treatment of the Spinozian attributes. The stakes in the discussion of the attributes should be clear. The objectivist interpretation of the attributes seems open to the critique from a phenomenological perspective that it implies an ide-

alist conception of ontology and thus precludes a theoretical practice, or
any real notion of practice. Deleuze's concerns, however, point in a very
different direction. The real danger, according to him, is that the attribute
of thought be given a priority over the other attributes, that the mind be
given priority over the body. This intellectualist conception of ontology
would not only destroy the univocity of being, but would also subordinate
any material and corporeal conception of being to the intellectual realm.
This discussion will necessarily be complex, and at points Deleuze's interpretation will seem strained with respect to Spinoza's text, but this complexity and this tension should only indicate to us how important this point
is for Deleuze's philosophy, how important it is to combat the privileges of
thought.

Deleuze articulates his idea of the equality of the attributes through a
theory of ontological parallelism.[13] The idea of a parallelism of the attributes should not be considered as another principle of being; rather, it is
simply a logical extension or development of the idea of the univocity of
being. If being is always and everywhere said in the same way, then the
attributes must be equal expressions. In other words, if, viewed from
above, univocity appears as the absolute uniformity of the whole, then
viewed from below it appears as the equal participation of all the constituent parts. We can identify three elements that constitute Deleuze's theory
of ontological parallelism: autonomy, equality, and unity.

The autonomy of the attributes should be understood foremost as a rejection of the Cartesian conception of the primacy of the mind over the
body. Spinoza claims, in opposition to Descartes, that the mind neither
controls nor suffers from the body, and similarly the body neither controls
nor suffers from the mind. There is a real separation between the attributes. Spinoza conceives the mind, then, as a "spiritual automaton"
(*Treatise on the Emendation of the Intellect* 85) because in thinking the
mind obeys only the laws of thought (cf. *Expressionism in Philosophy:
Spinoza* 140). The same, of course, must be said of the body: The body is
a corporeal automaton because in movement and rest the body obeys only
the laws of extension. This conception of the autonomy of the attributes
rests on one of the principles of efficient causality: Insofar as two things are
different, one cannot be the cause of the other (cf. *Ethics* IP3). The attributes, then, constitute independent series of cause and effect.

The proposition of parallelism, however, goes beyond a mere separation between the attributes. "The order and connection of ideas is *the same*
as the order and connection of things" (IIP7, emphasis mine). Spinoza's
proposition claims not only that the attributes are autonomous, but also
that they are organized in a parallel order: "And indeed, identity of connection means not only the autonomy of corresponding series, but an

isonomy, that is, an equality of principle between autonomous or independent series" (*Expressionism in Philosophy: Spinoza* 108). A second component of parallelism, then, is the establishment of an equality of principle among all the attributes, specifically between the two attributes accessible to us, thought and extension. This is the complete rejection of the Cartesian position: Not only is the body formally independent of the mind, but it is also equal to the mind in principle. We must understand equality of principle here in terms of ontological participation. The body and the mind both participate in being in autonomous and equal ways. Once again, this proposition follows directly from the principle of univocity: Corporeality and thought are equal expressions of being, said in the same voice.

We can already recognize that equality does not suffice to explain ontological parallelism. The different attributes are not only equal expressions of being; they are, in a certain sense, *the same expression*. In other words, the modes of the various attributes are the same from the point of view of substance.

> God produces things in all attributes at once: he produces them in the same order in each, and so there is a correspondence between modes of different attributes. But because attributes are really distinct this correspondence, or identity of order, excludes any causal action of one on another. Because the attributes are all equal, there is an identity of connection between modes differing in attribute. Because attributes constitute one and the same substance, modes that differ in attribute form one and the same modification. (110)

The substantial modification (*modificatio*) is the unity of modes that are produced in parallel in the different attributes by a single affection of substance. The concept of the modification itself is the demonstration of what Deleuze calls the *ontological* parallelism: The modes produced autonomously and equally in the different attributes appear as a unity from the point of view of substance in the form of the substantial modification (see *Spinoza: Practical Philosophy*). In Deleuze's interpretation, this theory of Spinozian parallelism functions not so much as an analysis of the organization of being,[14] but rather as a central lesson for speculation, one that will guide us throughout our study of the *Ethics*: Every proposition we affirm with regard to one of the attributes must be affirmed equally with regard to the other attribute. In other words, each time we recognize an aspect of the structure or function of the mind, we must ask ourselves how we can recognize a parallel structure or function of the body, and vice versa. (For example, if we are to affirm a certain nature of a true idea of the mind, we must also affirm a parallel nature of a true act of the body.)[15]

Deleuze's reading of ontological parallelism is an original interpretation in Spinoza studies. The beautiful simplicity of it consists in the fact that it follows very directly from the principle of univocity. If being is expressed always and everywhere in the same voice, then all its attributes must be structured as parallel expressions; the substantial unity of the modification, which straddles the different attributes, testifies to the univocity of being. Furthermore, the difficulties that we focused on earlier regarding the priority of thought in the foundation of the attribute seem to be resolved (or at least left behind) by the theory of the equality and ontological parallelism of the attributes. We should recognize, nonetheless, that while Deleuze's interpretation fits very well with the general spirit of Spinoza's ontological system, it does not agree with Spinoza's actual statement in Proposition 7: "The order and connection of ideas is the same as the order and connection of things" (IIP7). Deleuze recognizes that here Spinoza is not proposing an ontological parallelism, but rather an *epistemological* parallelism (99). This parallelism is not established equally among the various attributes, but rather it focuses primarily on the attribute of thought, establishing the relationship between an idea and its "object" ("res ideata, objectum ideae"). The problem is posed most clearly in the corollary of this proposition: "God's actual power of thinking is equal to its actual power of acting" (P7C). To appreciate the depth of this problem, we must keep in mind that "action" in Spinoza's terminology does not refer only to the movement and rest of the body, but equally to all the attributes. (See, for example, IIID3.). This formula of P7C, then, is proposing an equality, but not the equality of the mind and the body; on the contrary, the essence of thought (the power of thinking) is equated to the essence of being (the power of acting). Therefore, we are thrown back on the same problematic terrain of the subjectivist interpretation of the attribute.

Deleuze certainly recognizes this as a serious problem. Once again we are confronted by what seems to be a Spinozian tendency to privilege thought over the other attributes. The theory of epistemological parallelism, Deleuze claims, "forces us to confer on the attribute of thought a singular privilege: this attribute must contain as many irreducible ideas as there are modes of different attributes; still more, as many ideas as there are attributes. This privilege seems in flagrant contradiction with all the demands of ontological parallelism" (114). The privilege that seems to be accorded to thought here goes against the general design of the ontological system. In a first attempt to resolve this problem, Deleuze explains that in the scholium to this proposition Spinoza proceeds from the epistemological parallelism to the ontological parallelism, generalizing the case of thought (of the idea and its object) to all of the attributes. In this way, Deleuze proposes epistemological parallelism as secondary, as merely a "detour" (99) for reaching ontological parallelism, the more profound theory. This reading, however, is not very well substantiated in the text. The scholium is somewhat suggestive of ontological parallelism, but certainly does not state it clearly; the most suggestive supporting statement, in fact, is very weak: "I understand the same concerning the other attributes" (IIP7S). I do not think that this difficulty should draw into question Deleuze's proposal of an ontological parallelism—indeed, there is sufficient evidence elsewhere in Spinoza's work to support this thesis. The task here is to find a way to reconcile the two parallelisms so that they do not contradict one another; or better, to discover a way of avoiding the epistemological parallelism altogether.

Deleuze embarks, then, on a more involved discussion in order to address this task. The immediate object of this discussion is to rework the interpretation of the epistemological parallelism proposed in IIP7. The fundamental goal, though, which we should keep in mind throughout this complex argument, is to combat the privileges of thought and thereby preserve the ontological foundation of the philosophical framework. We must be careful, Deleuze begins, not to confuse the attributes of being with the powers of being: "The distinction of powers and attributes has an essential importance in Spinozism" (118). While being has an infinity of attributes, it has only two powers: the power to exist and act, and the power to think and know (103). The first power, the power to exist, is the *formal* essence of God. All the attributes participate equally in this essence, in the power to exist, as formally distinct expressions. This is a restatement of ontological parallelism. The second power, then, the power to think, is the *objective* essence of God. "God's absolute essence is formal in the attributes that constitute its nature, and objective in the idea that necessarily represents this nature" (120). The same attributes that are distinguished formally in God are distinguished objectively in the idea of God. This formulation of the two powers gives Deleuze the opportunity to combat the notion of the eminence of thought over the other attributes by subsuming the epistemological perspective within the ontological. "The attribute of thought is to the power to think what all attributes (including thought) are to the power to exist and act" (122). This slippage between powers and attributes sets the terms for a priority between the two powers. Even though Deleuze affirmed earlier that the powers are in some sense equal, here we find that the power to think (objective essence) is dependent on the power to exist (formal essence): "Objective being would amount to nothing did it not itself have a formal being in the attribute of thought" (122). Deleuze's claim of the priority of the ontological power (the power to exist) over the epistemological power (the power to think) thus preserves the equality among the attributes.

Finally, however, there arises yet another case in which it appears that thought is privileged over the other attributes. In the mind there are not only ideas that correspond to objects (*res ideata*), but also ideas of these ideas, and still other ideas of these ideas of ideas, and so on to infinity: "Whence this final apparent privilege of the attribute of thought, which is the ground of a capacity of ideas to reflect themselves ad infinitum. Spinoza sometimes says that the idea of an idea has to the idea the same relation as the idea to its object" (125). Before we enter into the details of this argument, which can easily seem tedious and arcane, we should try once again to clarify what is at stake here. Several commentators have argued that the problem of the idea of the idea in Spinoza is the problem of consciousness, or rather the problem of the reflection of the mind. Sylvain Zac, for example, poses the concept in this way: "Consciousness is the idea of the idea. It is united to the mind just as the mind is united to the body" (*L'idée de vie* 128; see also 121-28). Although Deleuze does not pose the issue in these terms, Zac's proposition makes clear the danger presented for Deleuze by this Spinozian example. The idea of the idea, as consciousness, seems to be constructing an interiority within the mind that, as Zac says, is united with the mind as the mind is united with the body. The principal threat of interiority in this case is the creation of a priority of the mind over the body and the subsumption of the dynamic of being within a mental dynamic of reflection. As we have seen several times, though, Deleuze is not a philosopher of consciousness: What this means is, on the one hand, that he maintains the priority of *ratio essendi* over *ratio cognoscendi*, and, on the other hand, that he refuses any subordination of the body to the mind. Therefore, it is quite clear that when Deleuze approaches this issue his main concern will be to preserve the ontological equality of the attributes. The basic problem, then, can be posed quite simply. While the idea and its object are conceived under two separate attributes, the idea of the idea and the idea are both conceived under the attribute of thought. What does it mean, then, to say that there is the same relationship between the idea and the object as there is between the idea of the idea and the idea? The claim that the two cases constitute the same relationship seems to give thought the capacity to subsume the relationship to all of the attributes within itself: Its priority as the attribute of reflection seems to give it the capacity to reproduce the inter-attribute dynamic completely within thought itself. The threat of an idealist perspective, a philosophy of consciousness, still haunts the Spinozian system.

Deleuze once again calls on the distinction of powers to address this difficulty: The two cases cannot be considered the same when considered from the point of view of attributes, he argues, but only when considered from the point of view of powers (110-11). In other words, the common relationship in the two cases should be explained by referring the first term to the formal power and the second to the objective power. The first case is very simple. The *res ideata*, as a mode of being (pertaining to one of the attributes), has a certain power to exist, and is thus an expression of formal essence. The idea of this object, however, refers not to the power to exist but to the power to think, and is thus an expression of objective essence. We can apply this same logic to the second case because an idea is also a mode of being. A mode of thought, just like a mode of any attribute, can be referred to the power to exist, as formal essence. When an idea is thus conceived, we can relate another idea to that idea, referring now to the power to think: This idea of the idea is an expression of objective essence. The common relationship that Spinoza is referring to, then, is that in each case the two terms refer to the two different powers: the power to exist and the power to think. This similarity, however, points to an important difference when we consider the two cases from the point of view of the attributes. In the first case, there is a formal distinction between an idea and its object because they are modes of different attributes. In the second case, though, between the idea of the idea and the idea, there is no formal distinction because they are both modes of thought.

> From this point of view we see the unity of an idea and the idea of that idea, insofar as they are given in God with the same necessity, *by the same power to think*. There is consequently only a conceptual distinction (*distinction de raison*) between the two ideas: the idea of an idea is the form of that idea, referred as such to the power to think. (126)

Deleuze is satisfied with this solution. He has answered the intellectualist challenge posed by consciousness by a reference to the different powers and, finally, to the ontological hierarchy of distinctions. The distinction involved in the dynamic of consciousness is not the real distinction that founds being, not the formal distinction that differentiates the attributes, but merely a conceptual distinction (*distinction de raison*). We can pose this clearly in Bergsonian terms: Consciousness does not mark a difference of nature, but merely a difference of degree. We have to admit, nonetheless, that the mind's capacity for reflection (consciousness, the idea of the idea) does give thought a certain privilege over the other attributes. Deleuze's argument, however, drawing on the different powers and distinctions, attempts to show that this privilege is ontologically insignificant.

Remark: From Forschung to Darstellung

In the previous section we analyzed several examples of Deleuze's effort to preserve the univocity of being on the basis of an ontological parallelism

among the attributes. The opponent in each case is an intellectualist reading of Spinoza's ontology, which at several points seems to give a real privilege to thought; Deleuze's strategy, which we have seen several times in
our study, is to subordinate *ratio cognoscendi* to *ratio essendi*. The Deleuzian arguments certainly have a very strong foundation in Spinoza's ontology, in the ontological parallelism of the attributes; nonetheless, these arguments appear weak when, in Spinoza's psychology and epistemology,
the problem of privilege continually reappears. To a certain extent, the
privileges of thought and the problem of the attributes should be explained as a residue of Cartesianism in Spinoza's thought, but this explanation is not sufficient on its own. The theory of the attributes remains a
problem in Deleuze's Spinoza.

Some readers of Spinoza, who, like Deleuze, recognize the centrality of
the univocity of being, have tried to resolve this problem by claiming an
evolution in Spinoza's thought: Antonio Negri, for example, argues that the
theory of the attributes disappears as Spinoza proceeds from the pantheistic utopia that characterizes the first phase of his thought, to the constitutive disutopia of his maturity. The attributes do indeed disappear from
the *Ethics* after Part II (with only a brief reappearance in Part V), and Negri
links this fact to historical evidence that Spinoza drafted the *Ethics* during
two distinct periods, from 1661 to 1665 and from 1670 to 1675 (*The Savage
Anomaly* 48). Negri argues, then, that Spinoza's philosophical transformation between these two periods precipitates the rejection of the attributes
(59). Negri's argument has come under serious critique, but it clearly
points to two issues that (even if we are to question his explanation) must
be addressed: The theory of the attributes remains problematic in the context of the Spinozian system, and the attributes are relatively absent from
the latter half of the *Ethics*.

It seems to me that there is an alternative or complementary explanation, available in Deleuze's work itself, to account for the disappearance of
the attributes. We could argue, consistently with Deleuze's interpretation, I
believe, that thought is privileged in the theory of the attributes only in
limited or accidental terms: Thought is the principal means of human speculation, and the theory of the attributes is linked to a mode of inquiry. If we
imagine that there is something substantial about the priority of thought
over the other attributes, we are merely confusing the form of our research
with the nature of being. The attributes appear in the *Ethics* not as a form of
being, but as a mode of inquiry, as a scientific *Forschung*. Marx makes clear
the distinction between *Forschung* and *Darstellung*, between the mode of
inquiry and the mode of presentation: "Of course the method of presentation [*Darstellung*] must differ in form from the method of inquiry [*Forschung*]. The latter has to appropriate the material in detail, to analyse its

different forms of development and to track down their inner connection. Only after this work has been done can the real movement be appropriately presented" (*Capital*, vol. 1, 102). Following this logic, the two phases of Spinoza's thought, which Negri proposes historically, can be identified with two moments or approaches in Spinoza's work.[16] The *Forschung* of the *Ethics*, the moment of speculation, relies on the theory of the attributes "to track down the inner connection" of being. Thought is given a certain priority in this moment, as the model of our speculation. "Only after this work has been done," Marx says, "can the real movement be appropriately presented." What does it mean to present appropriately the real movement of being? Here it means to present being as it makes itself, in the process of its constitution. In other words, only after the analytical moment has brought to light all the distinctions of the terrain can this same terrain be traversed a second time with a different bearing, with a practical attitude, appropriately presenting the "inner connections" and the "real movement" of being in the process of its own constitution. When the moment of research is complete, therefore, after Part II of the *Ethics*, the attributes no longer have a role and they drop out of the discussion. As we move forward in Spinoza's system of emendation, as we shift from speculation to practice, any priority of thought gradually disappears. In fact, Deleuze presents a powerful argument that Spinoza's theory of practice initially privileges the attribute of extension: The body is the model of practice. This seems to me, then, a consistent Deleuzian explanation of the questions of priority. In our research of being, in the moment of speculation, the mind plays the initial role of model; similarly, in Spinoza's *Darstellung*, in our practice of being, the body plays a parallel role.

How does Spinoza make this shift from *Forschung* to *Darstellung*, from speculation to practice? Deleuze's work makes clear that the hinge or the pivot that articulates these two moments is the thematic of power. Spinoza's discussion of power carries the developed ontological foundation onto the terrain of practice. It constitutes, as we claimed earlier, the fundamental passage, the Nietzschean transmutation: the hour of midnight. The speculative *Forschung* of power yields to its practical *Darstellung*. Let us turn our attention, then, to Spinoza's development of the thematic of power.

Power

3.6 The True and the Adequate

The question of the attributes has touched on Spinoza's epistemology, but really it has only scratched the surface. Thus far, we have treated Deleuze's defense against an intellectualist reading of Spinoza's epistemology. This defense rests primarily on a conception of ontological parallelism that is developed through an extension of the principle of univocity. Now we should turn to Deleuze's positive exposition of Spinozian epistemology, and specifically to Spinoza's proposal that we shift our attention from the true idea to the adequate idea as a more coherent and useful category of speculation. There is certainly a close relation between truth and being in Spinoza, but this nexus reveals not the intellectual character of being, but rather the ontological criteria of truth. We will see that Spinoza's discussion of adequacy brings the epistemological debate back to an ontological plane. The essential role in the argument is played by an ontological conception of the internal causality, or the singular production, of being. The adequate is defined as being: that which envelops and expresses its cause.

From one of his earliest works, the *Emendation of the Intellect*, Spinoza searches for an intrinsic definition of the true idea. Just as real being is cause of itself and gains its distinction from within, so too the true idea must be defined through an internal causality. According to Spinoza, as we have seen, the mind is a spiritual automaton that produces ideas autonomously, that is, with reference only to the attribute of thought. This basis provides Spinoza with a forceful critique of the traditional correspondence theory of truth that is implied by the epistemological parallelism discussed earlier: The true idea is the idea that agrees or corresponds with its object (*res ideata*). The correspondence theory, which poses merely a formal agreement, is blind to the production process and thus cannot fulfill Spinoza's initial criterion for the true idea: "The conception of truth as correspondence gives us no definition, either formal or material, of truth; it proposes a purely nominal definition, an extrinsic designation" (*Expressionism in Philosophy: Spinoza* 131). In epistemology, the extrinsic designation gives a weak conception of truth, just as in ontology the external cause provides a weak definition of being. The external definition, as we saw in the Bergson study, implies merely a "subsistent exteriority." (See Section 1.1.) We can already note from this critique of the correspondence theory that an ontological logic provides the foundation for Spinoza's epistemological investigation.

In this context, the Cartesian proposition of "clear and distinct" as the condition for truth provides us with a much more promising strategy because it addresses not only the form but also the content of the idea. Deleuze argues, however, that the conception of clear and distinct is insufficient for a Spinozian theory of truth in three respects. First, while the Cartesian proposition does succeed in referring to the content of the idea, this reference remains superficial as a "representative" content (132). The content of the clear and distinct idea cannot be a real content because "clear and distinct" does not recognize or comprehend the efficient cause of that idea. We know that since the mind is a spiritual automaton the proximate cause of any idea is always another idea, but the superficiality of representation is precisely its detachment from this cause. Second, the form of the clear and distinct idea also remains superficial in the form of a "psychological consciousness" (132). This Cartesian form does not attain the logical form of the idea that would explain the connection and order of ideas one to the other. The superficiality in this case is due to the detachment from the formal cause of the idea, which is precisely our power to think. Third, the Cartesian conception does not succeed in posing the unity of the content and the form of the true idea; in other words, Descartes does not recognize the spiritual automaton "that reproduces reality in producing ideas in their due order" (152). In short, the critiques of the "clear and distinct" strategy all spring from the fact that it attempts to define the true while only referring to the idea itself; the Cartesian strategy does not deal with the *causes* of ideas, and thus it cannot explain the process of their production. Once again, in the focus on causality and production, we can recognize Spinoza's ontological approach to truth. Deleuze relates this critique to his notion of expression: To be expressive, an idea must explain or envelop its cause. "A clear and distinct idea is still inexpressive, and remains unexplained. Good enough for recognition, but unable to provide a real principle of knowledge" (152-53). Precisely because of its failure to express or explain the true idea by means of its cause, the conception of truth as clear and distinct does not give us the terms to answer our fundamental questions: Where does truth come from and what can it do for us — or, as Nietzsche might ask, Why do we want truth? A Spinozian definition of truth must involve the expression of causality, production, and power.

The ontological critique of the clear and distinct idea prepares the terms for Spinoza's shift from the true idea to the adequate idea. The essential feature of Spinoza's conception of truth is the internal relation of an idea to its cause: "The adequate idea is precisely the idea as expressing its cause" (133, modified). We can contrast this with the Cartesian theory on all three points just presented. First, the adequate idea presents its content as the expression of its proximate efficient cause (another idea). Second, the form of the adequate idea is a logical form that is explained by its formal cause (the power to think): "The adequate idea is the idea that expresses its own cause and is explained by our own power" (151). Third, the content and the form of the adequate idea are united in the movement internal to the attribute of thought: "The spiritual automaton, manifested in the concatenation of ideas, is the unity of logical form and expressive content" (153). We can see Spinoza's insistence on replacing the Cartesian clear and distinct with his conception of adequateness as an ontologization of epistemology. "Spinoza's ontology is dominated by the notions of a cause of itself, in itself and through itself" (162). Spinoza's epistemology, too, is dominated by this same focus on causality: Truth, like being, is singular insofar as it envelops and expresses its own cause. Through the causal chain expressed by the adequate idea, through the move from the true to the adequate, Spinoza's epistemology takes on an ontological character. Spinoza's revolution in epistemology is to apply these same ontological criteria that define being as singular to the realm of truth. Along with Thomas Mark, a perceptive American commentator, Deleuze shows that Spinoza's theory of truth is a theory of "ontological truth."[17]

Adequate ideas are expressive, and inadequate ideas are mute.[18] In other words, the distinctive characteristic of an adequate idea is that it tells us something about the structure and connections of being (or at least the attribute of thought) through a direct expression of its efficient and formal causes. From an ontological perspective, the inadequate idea tells us nothing because we cannot recognize its place in the productive structure of thought; it is not situated in the dynamic causal mechanism of the spiritual automaton. One importance of the adequate idea, then, is that through the expression of its causes it increases our power of thought; the more adequate ideas we have, the more we know about the structure and connections of being, and the greater our power to think. Adequacy is infectious, giving rise to always greater expression. "Whatever ideas follow in the Mind from ideas that are adequate in the mind are also adequate" (IIP40). Spinoza, however, accompanies this claim with a realistic assessment of our condition. The vast majority of the ideas we have are inadequate ideas. At this point, it is obvious how Spinoza would answer the Nietzschean question posed earlier: We want truth, or rather adequacy, in order to increase our power to think. The strategy of the adequate idea makes the question of truth a project of power. Once the question of power enters the discussion, however, this epistemological discourse quickly transforms into an ethical project. "Spinoza asks: How do we come to form and produce adequate ideas, when we necessarily have so many inadequate ones that divert our power and separate us from what we can do?" (148, modified). Here, in this transformation of the epistemological toward the ethical, we see a combined application of the principle of singularity (an absolutely infinite being as cause of itself, the adequate idea as enveloping its cause) and the principle of power (being as productivity, truth as creation); the principle of singularity gives us the terms for the definition of the adequate idea, and the principle of power transforms this definition into a project.

Before moving on, let us pause for a moment to recognize the importance of ontological parallelism and its relation to the Spinozian concep-

tion of adequacy. We claimed earlier that if we are to maintain Deleuze's
conception of ontological parallelism, then in principle the character or
movement of one attribute must in some sense correspond to that of the
other attributes, because fundamentally all of them refer equally to the
character or movement of being. The concept of truth presents an interesting test for this theory. Following a Cartesian theory, for example, we
would be forced to pose, parallel to our conception of a clear and distinct
idea or a clear and distinct action of the mind, some conception of a clear
and distinct action of the body. Since Cartesian truth does not account for
movement and production, it is not easily applicable to the corporeal
plane. Spinozian adequacy, on the other hand, since it refers to the nature
of being itself and to the genealogy of its production, applies to all the attributes equally: Just like an adequate action of the mind, an adequate action of the body is expressive in that it explains or envelops its cause. The
adequate is that which discloses the productive dynamic of being.

3.7 What a Body Can Do

With the conception of adequacy, Spinoza is able to develop the epistemological framework to the point where he can pose an initial ethical question, an initial question of power. One aspect of the very steep path that
Spinoza is leading us on will direct us to proceed from inadequate ideas to
adequate ones. We can easily pose this ethical goal more generally as the
increase of our power to think, or more generally still as the increase of
our power to exist and act: How can we increase our power to exist, or, in
theological terms, how can we approach God (the infinite power to exist
and act)? At this point, however, with only an epistemological foundation,
we have very little idea how this operation is possible; we are still far from
being able to embark on an ethical practice. In fact, posing the ethical
question in such grand terms is empty and pointless without some specific
and concrete means of addressing our goal.

A further moment of speculation is needed. Spinoza uses the mind as
the primary model of speculation; now we have to shift our concentration
to the body, from epistemology to physics, because it is the body that will
reveal a model of practice. "Spinoza does seem to admit that we have to
pass through an empirical study of bodies in order to know their relations,
and how they are composed" (212). We will see, however, in the long passage from physics to ethics, that the criterion of adequacy, of expressing or
enveloping the cause, remains central to the development of Spinoza's argument. Spinozian physics is an empirical investigation to try to determine
the laws of the interaction of bodies: the encounters of bodies, their composition and decomposition, their compatibility (or composability), and

their conflict. A body is not a fixed unit with a stable or static internal structure. On the contrary, a body is a dynamic relationship whose internal
structure and external limits are subject to change. What we identify as a
body is merely a temporarily stable relationship (IIP13Def).[19] This proposition of the dynamic nature of bodies, of the continual flux of their internal dynamic, allows Spinoza a rich understanding of the interaction among
bodies. When two bodies meet, there is an encounter between two dynamic relationships: Either they are indifferent to each other, or they are
compatible and together compose a new relationship, a new body; or,
rather, they are incompatible and one body decomposes the relationship
of the other, destroying it, just as a poison decomposes the blood (cf. Letter
32 to Henry Oldenberg). This physical universe of bodies at motion and
rest, in union and conflict, will provide the context in which we can delve
deeper into the functioning and structure of power: "In order to really
think in terms of power, one must first pose the question in relation to the
body" (257). Spinoza's physics are the cornerstone of his ethics.

Deleuze is fascinated by a passage in one of the early scholia of Book III:
"No one has yet determined what the Body can do. . . . For no one has yet
come to know the structure of the Body so accurately that he could explain
all its functions" (IIIP2S). The question of power (what a body can do) is
immediately related to the internal structure of the body. This charts the
initial direction of our investigation: To understand the nature of power,
we must first discover the internal structure of the body, we must decompose the unity of the body according to its lines of articulation, its differences of nature. Deleuze reminds us that the investigation of this structure
must be conducted not in terms of the power to act (spontaneity), but
rather in terms of the power to be affected: "A body's structure is the composition of its relation. What a body can do is the nature and the limits of its
power to be affected" (218). The horizon of affectivity, then, will provide
the terrain for our speculation and reveal further distinctions within the
body, distinctions within power.

On a first level in our model of power, we find that the power to be
affected is filled by active affections and passive affections. The importance
of this distinction is clear: To the extent that our power to be affected is
filled by active affections, it relates directly to our power to act, but to the
extent that it is filled by passive affections, it relates only to our power to
feel or suffer (*puissance de pâtir*). Passive affections really mark our lack of
power. Once again, the essential logic of the argument refers to expression
and production: The active is distinct from the passive in its relation to the
cause. "Our force of suffering *affirms* nothing, because it *expresses* nothing
at all: it 'envelops' only our impotence, that is to say, *the lowest degree of
our power to act*" (224, modified). We said earlier that the power to be

affected demonstrates the plenitude of being in that it is always completely filled with active and passive affections; yet the power to be affected only appears as plenitude from the physical point of view. From the ethical point of view, on the contrary, the power to be affected varies widely according to its composition. To the extent that it is filled with passive affections, it is reduced to its minimum, and to the extent that it is filled with active affections, it is increased to its maximum. "Whence the importance of the ethical question. *We do not even know what a body can do*, Spinoza says. That is: *We do not even know of what affections we are capable, nor the extent of our power*. How could we know this in advance?" (226). This, then, is the first order of business in preparing the terrain for an ethical project: Investigate what affects we are capable of, discover what our body can do.

Spinoza's theory of *conatus* (or striving) marks precisely the intersection of production and affection that is so important to Deleuze: "The variations of *conatus* as it is determined by this or that affection are the dynamic variations of our power to act" (231). *Conatus* is the physical instantiation of the ontological principle of power. On one hand, it is the essence of being insofar as being is productive; it is the motor that animates being as the world. To this extent, *conatus* is Spinoza's continuation of the legacy of Renaissance naturalism: Being is spontaneity, pure activity. On the other hand, however, *conatus* is also the instantiation of the ontological principle of power in that *conatus* is a sensibility; it is driven by not only the actions, but also the passions, of the mind and the body (see, for example, IIIP9). It is this rich synthesis of spontaneity and affectivity that marks the continuity between the ontological principle of power and *conatus*.

At this point the ethical project requires a moment of empirical realism. When Spinoza begins to take stock of the state of our body, of our power, he notes that, by necessity, our power to be affected is largely filled by passive affections. God, or Nature, is completely filled with active affections, because there is no cause external to it. However, "the force by which a man perseveres in existing is limited, and infinitely surpassed by the power of external causes" (IVP3). To the extent that our power is surpassed by the power of Nature as a whole, to the extent that external forces are more powerful than our own forces, we will be filled with passive affections. Now, since passive affections largely constitute our existence, we should focus our investigation on these affections to see if we can make meaningful distinctions among them.

Within the domain of extension, passive affections are characterized by encounters between our body and other bodies—encounters that can appear as random because they are not caused by us. The order of passions, then, is the order of chance encounters, of the *fortuitus occursus* (238). A simple encounter between two bodies, however, poses an extremely rich and complex scene for analysis, because one body itself is not a fixed unit with a static structure, but rather a dynamic relationship whose internal structure and external limits are open and continually subject to change. As we noted earlier, what Spinoza identifies as a body or an individual is simply a temporarily stable assemblage of coordinated elements (*Ethics* IIP13Def). An encounter between two bodies, then, will be characterized by the composability or the incomposability of their two relationships. Now, given this dynamic conception of bodies and their interactions, Deleuze proposes two cases of chance encounters that will allow us to distinguish two types of passive affections, and thus descend one more level in our model of power. In the first case, I meet a body whose internal relationship is compatible with the internal relationship of my body, and thus the two bodies together compose a new relationship. We can say, then, that this external body "agrees with my nature" or that it is "good" or "useful" for me. Furthermore, this encounter produces an affection in me that itself agrees with or is good for my nature: It is a joyful encounter in that it increases my power to act. The first case of chance encounter, then, results in a joyful passive affection because it presents a "composable" relationship and thus increases my power to act. In the second case of chance encounter, though, I meet a body whose internal relationship is not compatible with that of my body; this body does not agree with my nature. Either one body will decompose the relationship of the other or both bodies will be decomposed. In either case, the important fact is that there will be no increase of power, because a body cannot gain power from something that does not agree with it. Since this encounter results in a decrease of power, the affection produced by it is sadness. Actual encounters, of course, are more complicated than either of these two limit cases: There may be different degrees of partial compatibility and partial conflict in an encounter, or, further, the affects can combine in a myriad of ways (the sadness of what I hate brings me joy, etc.). These two cases, however, joyful passive affections and sad passive affections, provide us with the limit cases of possible encounters, and thus they allow us to posit a further distinction, describing a second level in our model of power.

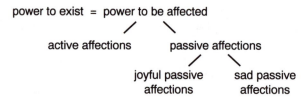

It is once again time for a moment of Spinoza's realism. What is the relative frequency of joyful and sad encounters? In principle, or rather in the abstract, humans agree in nature, and thus human encounters ought to be purely joyful. However, this is only true to the extent that our power to be affected is filled by active affections. "Insofar as men are subject to passions, they cannot be said to agree in nature" (IVP32). Therefore, in reality, humans agree very little with one another, and the large majority of chance encounters are sad.

At each point in the investigation of the structure of the body where we have recognized a distinction, we have also recognized that the human condition lies largely on the weak side of the equation: Our power to be affected is filled largely by passive affections rather than active affections; and, further, our passive affections are constituted largely by sad passive affections rather than joyful passive affections. One could easily be disheartened at this point by Spinoza's pessimistic appraisal of the human condition—but that would be to miss the point of the project. The investigation of the internal structure of power and the realistic evaluation of our condition are oriented toward refining the ethical question so that it can provide the basis for an ethical practice; what may appear as pessimism is Spinoza's practical perspective. To appreciate the richness of this approach, consider the typical Nietzschean ethical mandate: Become active. How can such an ethical proposition be transformed into an ethical practice? In other words, through Nietzsche we can clearly recognize the desire, the power (and in this sense the good) of becoming active, but we find no means to follow it through in practice. Spinoza too recognizes ethics as an issue of becoming active, but he delves one step deeper to enrich that ethical perspective. "The ethical question falls then, in Spinoza, into two parts: *How can we come to produce active affections?* But first of all: *How can we come to experience a maximum of joyful passions?* (246). Through the investigation of power, Spinoza has now prepared the terrain for the conversion from speculation to practice that will set his ethics in motion.

Practice

3.8 Common Notions: The Assemblages of Composable Being

Through Spinoza's investigation of the structure of power and his realistic estimation of the human condition we have arrived at the limit of speculation. The human condition resides principally in the point of the minimum of power; when we adopt this position, we can adopt too a truly ethical position. This is the end of speculation and the beginning of practice;

this is the moment of transmutation—the hour of midnight. Spinozian speculation has illuminated the terrain of power, defined its primary structures; now, we must convert this speculative dynamic into a practical project. How can we effect this transmutation? Where can we find the impetus to put a practical project in motion? A first hint that Deleuze gives us is that we must shift our focus from affirmation to joy. "The sense of joy appears as the properly ethical sense; it is to practice what affirmation itself is to speculation" (272). Joy, in other words, is the affirmation of being in the moment of its practical constitution; our increase of power is the affirmative constitution of being itself. It is not immediately evident, however, how our practice can begin with joy. Just like Nietzsche's ethical mandate "become active," so too a Spinozian mandate such as "become joyful" lacks the mechanism by which to initiate a practical project. Deleuze attempts another tack, presenting the project in negative form, to give it a more practical thrust: The first practical task of the *Ethics*, he claims, is to combat sadness: "The devaluation of sad passions, and the denunciation of those who cultivate and depend on them, form the practical object of philosophy" (270; see also *Spinoza: Practical Philosophy* 25-29). We have already noted, though, that in reality most of our passions are sad passions, that most chance encounters among bodies are incompatible and destructive. How can we begin a practice of joy from such a state? The attack on sadness still lacks an initial practical key.

We should begin instead by looking more closely at Spinoza's physics of bodies: "No one has yet come to know the structure [*fabrica*] of the Body so accurately that he could explain all its functions" (IIIP2S). What does Spinoza mean by structure? "It is a system of relations between the parts of a body," Deleuze explains. "By inquiring how these relations vary from one body to another, we have a way of directly determining the resemblances between two bodies, however disparate they may be" (278). Our investigation of the structure or relationships that constitute the body allows us to recognize common relationships that exist between our body and another body. An encounter between our body and this other body will necessarily be joyful, because the common relationship guarantees a compatibility and the opportunity to compose a new relationship, thereby increasing our power. Precisely in this way the analysis of bodies allows us to begin a practical project. By recognizing similar compositions or relationships among bodies, we have the criteria necessary for a first ethical selection of joy: We are able to favor compatible encounters (joyful passions) and avoid incompatible encounters (sad passions). When we make this selection, we are producing common notions: "A common notion is always an idea of a similarity of composition in existing modes" (275). The formation of the common notion constitutes the first step of an ethical practice.

This conception of the production of common notions, however, is not yet precise enough to be practical. We must make a distinction, Deleuze explains, between common notions that are more universal and common notions that are less universal. The most universal common notions are those that recognize a similarity from a very general point of view: They may involve, at the extreme, what is common to all bodies, such as extension, motion, and rest. These very universal common notions, however, are precisely those that are least useful to us. On the other hand, the least universal common notions are in fact those that immediately present us with the greatest utility. These notions are those that represent a similar composition between two bodies that directly agree with each other, from their own local points of view. Just as we continually descended within the internal structure of power, here too we must descend to the lowest, most local, level of commonality to initiate our practical project. "Through such notions we understand agreements between modes: they go beyond an external perception of agreements observed by chance, to find in a similarity of composition an internal and necessary reason for an agreement of bodies" (276). We can see, then, especially in the most specific of cases, that the common notion discovers an internal logic, that the common notion envelops and explains its cause, or, in other words, that the common notion is an adequate idea: "Common notions in general are necessarily adequate; in other words, common notions are ideas that are formally explained by our power to think and that, materially, express the idea of God as their efficient cause" (279). The common notion provides us the means to construct for ourselves an adequate idea.

The first adequate idea we can have is the recognition of something in common between two bodies; this adequate idea immediately leads to another adequate idea—in this way, we can begin our constructive project to become active. Deleuze, however, is not yet satisfied that we have presented this initial moment in sufficiently practical terms: "There is, though, a danger that the common notion might appear to intervene like a miracle, unless we explain how we come to form it. . . . Precisely, how do we form (common notions), in what favorable circumstances? How do we arrive at our power to act?" (280-81). When we consider the Spinozian theory of common notions, Deleuze warns us, we should be careful to avoid two dangerous interpretative errors. The first error with respect to the common notions would be "overlooking their biological sense in favor of their mathematical sense" (281). In other words, we should remember that common notions refer principally to a physics of bodies, not a logic of thought: We would do better to locate them as rising up from a Hobbesian material terrain, rather than from a Cartesian mathematical universe. The second interpretative error we might make with respect to the common notions would be "overlooking their practical function in favor of their speculative content" (281). When common notions are first introduced in Book II of the *Ethics*, they are introduced precisely in their logical order, from the speculative point of view. This speculative presentation regards the commons notions as moving from the most universal (motion, rest, etc.) toward the least universal. The practical progression of common notions in Book V is exactly the opposite: We move from the least universal (a specific compatible relationship between two bodies) toward the most universal. Common notions are not primarily a speculative form of analysis, but a practical tool of constitution.

Here, to begin the practical progression, we can assume that by chance we experience a compatible encounter. We can translate the famous epistemological point of departure of Spinoza's *Emendation of the Intellect*, "habemus enim ideam verum" (we have a true idea, or we have at least one true idea), to the realm of bodies and passions: "habemus enim affectionem passam laetam" (we have at least one joyful passive affection). This experience of joy is the spark that sets the ethical progression in motion: "When we encounter a body that agrees with our own, when we experience a joyful passive affection, we are induced to form the idea of what is common to that body and our own" (282). The process begins with the experience of joy. This chance encounter with a compatible body allows us, or induces us, to recognize a common relationship, to form a common notion. There are two processes going on here, however, which Deleuze insists must be kept distinct. In the first moment, we strive to avoid the sad passions that diminish our power to act and accumulate joyful passions. This effort of selection does increase our power, but never to the point of becoming active: Joyful passions are always the result of an external cause; they always indicate an inadequate idea. "We must then, *by the aid of joyful passions*, form the idea of what is common to some external body and our own. For this idea alone, this common notion, is adequate" (283). The first moment, the accumulation of joyful passions, prepares the condition for this leap that provides us with an adequate idea.

Let us look more closely at this second moment, at the "leap" from the joyful passion to the common notion. How do we make this leap? How do we make an encounter adequate? We know that joy is the experience of an affection that agrees with our nature, an affection that increases our power. The same joy is constituted by a joyful passive affection and a joyful active affection; the only difference is that a joyful passion arises from an external cause, while a joyful action arises from an internal cause: "When Spinoza suggests that what agrees with reason may also be born of it, he means that from every passive joy there may arise an active joy distinguished from it only by its cause" (274-75). The passage from passive joy to active joy involves substituting an internal cause for an external cause; or, more precisely, it involves enveloping or comprehending the cause within the encounter itself. This corporeal logic is parallel to the epistemological logic of adequacy that we discussed earlier. The new encounter is adequate (and active) because it expresses its own cause; that is, it expresses the common relationship between two bodies. This operation of enveloping the cause, however, still remains obscure until we recognize that a joyful passion presents us necessarily with a situation of commonality: A joyful passion can only arise from an external body that is composed of a relationship common to our body. When our mind forms an idea of the common relationship shared between this body and our body (a common notion), the joyful affection ceases to be passive and becomes active: "It is distinct from the passive feeling from which we began, but distinct only in its cause: its cause is no longer an inadequate idea of an object that agrees with us, but the necessarily adequate idea of what is common to that object and ourselves" (284). This process of enveloping or comprehending the cause of an encounter allows Spinoza to claim that "an affect which is a passion ceases to be a passion as soon as we form a clear and distinct idea of it" (VP3). This process of enveloping the cause, then, constitutes the "leap" to action and adequacy.

The common notions constitute for Deleuze the "ontological rupture" of Spinoza's thought that marks the completion of the transformation from speculation to practice. "Common notions are one of the fundamental discoveries of the *Ethics*" (292; see also *Spinoza: Practical Philosophy*, chapter 5, in particular 114ff.). With the establishment of the practical perspective, Spinoza has provided a radically new vision of ontology. Being can no longer be considered a given arrangement or order; here being is the assemblage of composable relationships. We should keep in mind, however, that the essential element for ontological constitution remains the Spinozian focus on causality, on being's "productivity" and "producibility." The common notion is the assemblage of two composable relationships to create a new, more powerful relationship, a new, more powerful body—this assemblage, however, is not merely a chance composition but an ontological constitution, because the process envelops the cause within the new body itself. We are suddenly thrown back to the opening definition of the *Ethics*—"Per causa sui intelligo ... "—but now we read it with an entirely different attitude. *Causa sui*, cause of itself, has acquired a new, practical meaning. The essential characteristic of Spinozian ontological constitution is adequacy, that is, the expression of the causal chain of being. The practical strategy of the formation of common notions, of ontological assemblages, has forged the ontological investigation into an ethical project: Become active, become adequate, become being. Spinozian practice is beginning to climb up the same ladder that the analysis of Spinozian speculation has constructed moving downward. Constitutive practice defines the productive series: joyful passive affections → common notions → active affections.

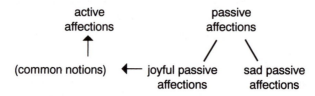

Speculation has mapped the terrain of power, and now practice is inhabiting that terrain, breathing life into its internal structure. Practice is moving upward, constructing the relations of being from below. The driving motor that animates this entire operation is *conatus*: When Spinozian physics is transported to an ethical plane, we no longer see simply bodies in motion and rest, but rather we find bodies infused with desire. As we move from sadness to joy, from passions to actions, we are discovering the path of the increase of our power. We should continually keep in mind that this path of corporeal and spiritual emendation is not simply presented as a vague ethical mandate; when Spinoza poses "becoming active" as a goal, he also presents the practical means of attaining this goal. "There is a whole learning process involved in common notions, in our *becoming active*: we should not overlook the importance in Spinozism of the problem of an educational process" (288). The Spinozian path to beatitude is an apprenticeship in power, an education in virtue.

3.9 The Constitution of Reason

Spinozian practice always begins with the body as model. However, while the common notions set off from a corporeal domain, they also construct a theory of ideas that is parallel to the theory of bodies. This constitutive epistemology that we find in the beginning of Part V of the *Ethics* is radically different from the given, preformed epistemology presented in Part II, and this difference is due in large part to the conversion from speculation to practice accomplished on the corporeal plane in Parts III and IV:

> In Part Two of the *Ethics* Spinoza considers the speculative content of common notions; he supposes them given or potentially given. ... At the opening of Part Five he analyzes the practical function of common notions, supposed given; this function consists in the common notion

being the cause of an adequate idea of an affection, that is, of an active
joy. (286)

The two epistemological arguments share the same categories and terminology, but they approach the topic from different perspectives, with different attitudes. In Part II, in the speculative moment, Spinoza laid out the
mathematical and logical order of the three different kinds of ideas, but in
Part V Spinoza's practical perspective puts this epistemological order in
motion. The common notion, recognized now as a constructive agent, as
an assemblage, is the mechanism by which the mind moves from a passion
to an action, from an inadequate idea to an adequate idea, from imagination to reason. The formation of common notions is the practical constitution of reason.

The theory that epistemology can be constituted in practice rests on a
notion of the materiality of the intellect that solidly locates Spinozian
thought both philosophically in the materialist tradition and historically in
the age of the birth of modern industry. An early passage from the *Emendation of the Intellect* discussing the method of improving our minds illustrates these connections very clearly:

> Matters here stand as they do with corporeal tools. . . . Just as men, in the
> beginning, were able to make the easiest things with the tools they were
> born with (however laboriously and imperfectly), and once these had
> been made, made other, more difficult things with less labor and more
> perfectly, and so, proceeding gradually from the simplest works to tools,
> and from tools to other works and tools, reached the point where they
> accomplished so many and so difficult things with little labor, in the same
> way the intellect, by its inborn power, makes intellectual tools for itself,
> by which it works still other tools, or the power of searching further, and
> so proceeds by stages, until it reaches the pinnacle of wisdom.
> (*Emendation of the Intellect* 30-31)

The mind forges the common notion from inadequate ideas, just as the
body forges a hammer from iron. The common notion serves as a practical
tool in our effort toward the pinnacle of wisdom.

This practical and material perspective provides a new foundation and a
new dynamic of movement for Spinoza's system of the different kinds of
knowledge: the first kind (imagination, opinion, and revelation), the second kind (reason), and the third kind (intuition). Spinoza directs us to analyze the lowest kind of knowledge in the same way that he insisted we
focus on the passions. First, he operates a devaluation: "Knowledge of the
first kind is the only cause of falsity, whereas knowledge of the second and
of the third kind is necessarily true" (*Ethics* IIP41). However, just as we
have seen with regard to the passions, once Spinoza operates this devalu-

ation he also adopts a realistic attitude and claims that the vast majority of our ideas reside in the first kind of knowledge. Those philosophers who persuade themselves that humans can live strictly by the dictates of reason, Spinoza is fond of saying, end up simply cursing and bemoaning, rather than understanding, human nature. We cannot simply exclude or negate the first kind of knowledge, but rather we must use it as our point of departure. The practical project of epistemology, then, is the movement from the first to the second and third kinds of knowledge. At this point, Spinoza can reassess the value of the first kind of knowledge with a different attitude: Even though it is the only source of falsity, the first kind of knowledge is nonetheless composed of ideas that *may be true*.

This revalorization does not yet give us a practical point of departure. At this point, just as we have recognized the distinction between joyful passions and sad passions, we must discover a relevant distinction within the first kind of knowledge. What imagination, opinion, and revelation have in common is that in each an idea is characterized by signs rather than by expression; in other words, an idea of the first kind depends on an external rather than an internal cause, and is thus inadequate. However, unlike the other two forms, imagination arises from the chance encounters between bodies: "This knowledge is obtained through 'vague experience' [*experientia vaga*], and 'vague' relates, etymologically, to the accidental character of encounters" (289). Spinozian imagination is a material imagination in that it provides the possibility of reading the commonality and conflict in the encounters among bodies. Since it operates on the material plane, where constitutive relationships are possible, the imagination presents us with *indicative* signs. On this terrain, the analysis can open up to the consideration of common notions and composable relationships. On the other hand, the other two forms of the first kind of knowledge, opinion and revelation, present no corporeal encounter, but merely opaque mandates: They merely provide us with *imperative* signs. The causes of these ideas remain obscure to us, and thus they cannot indicate the real genealogy of their formation, their real productive structure. Therefore, while all of the ideas of the first kind may be true, the imagination is distinguished from opinion and revelation because an idea that arises from the material field of imagination gives indications of its cause. In other words, since the imagination presents us with corporeal relationships, it is open to the laws of composability. The imagination not only may be true, but, through the indication of its cause, it *may be adequate*.

The common notion demonstrates the practical force of this distinction and puts it in motion. "If we consider their origin, common notions find in imagination the very conditions of their formation. If we consider their practical function, moreover, they apply only to things that can be imagined" (294). Common notions, as assemblages, are the practical pivot; they are building blocks that arise on the terrain of the imagination to constitute reason. The production of common notions shows that there is what Deleuze calls a "curious harmony" between the imagination and reason. Through the common notion, imagination and reason are linked on a continuum as different stages or planes in the process of intellectual constitution. However, there remains a real difference between them. The imagination begins by affirming the presence of an object, but no matter how strong or intense an imagination may be, we continue to regard the imagined object as present in a possible or contingent way. The specific property of reason is to consider things as necessary. The common notion, then, transforms the fluctuation and contingency of imagination into the permanence and consistency of reason: "An affect which arises from reason is necessarily related to the common properties of things, which we always regard as present ... and which *we always imagine in the same way*" (VP7Dem, emphasis mine). Here reason is presented as an intensified imagination that has gained the power to sustain its imagining by means of the construction of the common notion. "Necessity, presence and frequency are the three characteristics of common notions" (296). Reason is the imagination that returns, the refrain.

Earlier, we found that the central difference between the joyful passive affection and the joyful active affection is the external cause of the former and the internal cause of the later. The common notion operates the transformation, maintaining the affection while enveloping or comprehending the cause. Here, in the epistemological domain, we are presented with a corresponding framework of constitution through assemblage. The imagination, like the joyful passion, is the condition that allows us to begin the process. The central difference between the imagination and reason is the contingency of the former and the necessity of the latter. The common notion operates the transformation that makes the imagination permanent; it is the passage to reason. Therefore, we can plot an epistemological construction parallel to our earlier diagram of the structure of the affects. A constitutive epistemological practice is defined by the series: imagination → common notion → reason.

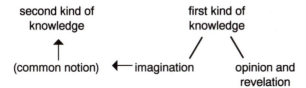

The keystone of Spinoza's revolution in epistemology is his conception of the role of the common notion as the link between imagination and reason. Spinoza demystifies reason. In the speculative argument of Part II, reason was defined in a Cartesian, mathematical spirit. Reason was a *given* system of necessary truth, and thus the production of reason was completely obscure. Therefore, the first kind of knowledge, the source of all error, could play no positive role in a project for truth; the only strategy could be its negation. Now, in the practical moment of Spinoza's thought, we find an important distinction between the different forms of the first kind of knowledge and a valorization of the imagination. The imagination provides a real (if fluctuating and contingent) indication of the state of bodies and relationships that are present. The common notion intervenes with the capacity to make our imagining permanent and necessary: The assemblage does not negate the imagination, but instead carries it to the plane of reason. The operation of the common notion makes clear that the Spinozian process of constitution is not at all dialectical. The progressive movement to a further stage is not accomplished through the negation of the present stage, but rather through its composition, preserving it with greater intensity and substance. In this context, contingency and necessity, imagination and reason are not exclusive and opposing couples, but rather they are plateaus linked together on a productive continuum by the process of constitution.

Remark: Theoretical Practice and Practical Constitution

Now that we have articulated the basic elements of Deleuze's conception of practice in Spinozian philosophy, we can return to Althusser and reconsider the strength of the phenomenological critique we posed earlier. The crux of the issue, from the perspective of our study, is the relationship between speculation (or theory) and practice. We have seen that Deleuze reads Spinoza as an extended drama dealing with the form of this relationship: In the first sections of the *Ethics*, Spinoza investigates being from a speculative perspective and discovers the fundamental ontological principles; later, from a practical perspective, Spinoza leads us toward a real constitution of being in corporeal and epistemological terms. One of the most important contributions of Deleuze's interpretation is to discover and clarify these two related moments in Spinoza's thought: speculation and practice. On this specific point, we may be tempted to say that the positions presented by Althusser and Deleuze are finally not so distant because, in certain regards, Althusser presents a similar relationship between theory and practice.

First we find that theory draws from practice: "Posing and resolving our theoretical problem ultimately consists in theoretically expressing the 'solution,' *existing in the practical state*, that Marxist practice has given" (*For Marx* 165, modified). Inversely, practice is dependent on theory. This is best expressed by one of Althusser's favorite quotations from Lenin: "Without theory, no revolutionary practice" (166). Reading Deleuze's Spinoza, we have also developed a certain interdependent relationship between theory and practice. Ontological speculation prepares the terrain for a constitutive practice; or rather, after ontological speculation (as *Forschung*) has brought to light the distinctions of the terrain, this same terrain is traversed a second time in a different direction, with a different bearing, with a practical attitude (as *Darstellung*), presenting the "inner connections" and the "real movement" of being in the process of its own constitution. In an interview with Michel Foucault, Deleuze gives a slightly different, but I think compatible explanation of this relationship, as a series of relays between theory and practice: "Practice is a set of relays from one theoretical point to another, theory is a relay from one practice to another. No theory can develop without eventually encountering a wall, a practice is necessary for piercing this wall" ("Intellectuals and Power" 206). Thus, using this image of relays, we can give a Deleuzian reading to Lenin's insight. "Without theory, no revolutionary practice": Without theory there is no terrain on which practice can arise, just as inversely, without practice, there is no terrain for theory. Each provides the conditions for the existence and development of the other.

When we look more closely, however, at Althusser's conception of the relationship between theory and practice, we find a fundamental difference that is often masked, but always present, in his work. The interrelation between theory and practice in Althusser always concedes, in the final instance, a priority to theory; practice is continually undermined, recuperated, subsumed. Consider, for example, how Althusser interprets Lenin's motto: " 'Without theory, no revolutionary practice.' Generalizing it: theory is essential to practice" (*For Marx* 166). Althusser's extension of Lenin involves an important modification. The relation between theory and practice in Lenin's motto could be read as a relationship of equality, but Althusser poses theory as primary, as the essence of practice. The October Revolution gives Althusser a concrete example: "The practice of the Bolshevik Party was based on the dialectic in *Capital*, on Marxist 'theory' " (175). The primacy given to theory here allows Althusser to subsume practice within theory itself. Although, of course, there are other forms of practice, Althusser's analysis always tends to focus on "theoretical practice" as the central political form, the archetype of practice. Theoretical practice is a synthesis of theory and practice, but a synthesis that always maintains the priority of theory.

Even when, years later, Althusser is addressing this position as a problem, in the spirit of self-criticism, he does not substantially modify this essential relation between theory and practice. Althusser claims to want to correct the "theoreticist" error (*Essays in Self-Criticism* 105, 128, 142) that skewed his analysis, and, specifically, he sees the need to revise his "theory of theoretical practice," which represented the culminating point of this theoreticist tendency (147). Here, as always, however, Althusser is very subtle in his self-criticism. When he seems to be modifying a past position, his argument serves instead to reinforce that same position. His self-criticism of the theory of theoretical practice functions in exactly this way: "In *theoretically* overestimating philosophy, I underestimated it *politically*, as those who correctly accused me of not 'bringing in' the class struggle were quick to point out" (150). We have to read this sentence very carefully. Althusser has been criticized (correctly) for not having given sufficient importance to the class struggle as a force of political practice. Accepting this critique, he reframes the discussion of theory and practice in terms of philosophy. His error was to misjudge philosophy—in overestimating philosophy theoretically, he underestimated it politically. He must extend his understanding of philosophy to appreciate its practical, political power. On this basis, he gives a (new?) definition of the theory-practice relationship. Philosophy is "politics in theory," or, more specifically, "philosophy is, in the last instance, class struggle in theory" (150). Social practice is present, but only insofar as it is *within theory*. The displacement of the problem to philosophy allows Althusser to subsume practice within theory once again as a secondary and dependent element.

Deleuze's view of the relationship between theory and practice, in contrast, emphasizes that the two activities remain autonomous and equal in principle. In Deleuze there is no synthesis of theory and practice, and no priority of one over the other. We have shown at great length that, in effect, Deleuze poses the primary condition for a materialist philosophy as the critique of any "theoreticist tendency," of any privileging of thought. (See Sections 3.4 and 3.5.) Let us propose, then, as a first approximation, that theory relates to practice as the activity of the mind relates to the activity of the body, with no direct causal relationship and no priority between the two. "The Body cannot determine the Mind to thinking, and the Mind cannot determine the Body to motion, to rest or to anything else (if there is anything else)" (*Ethics* IIIP2). We should keep in mind, of course, that there is not an identity between the two couples mind/body and theory/practice: Our speculation investigates the principles of being equally in the domain of thought and that of extension; similarly, the practical constitution of being involves both the mind and the body. The common relationship we are pointing to is the autonomy and equality of the terms in each couple. In this sense, Deleuze can imagine the relationship as a series of relays. It might even make sense in this context to speak of a theoretical automaton and a practical automaton as expressions that equally refer back to the power of being.

These arguments for autonomy, however, should be read above all as polemical positions. Just as Spinoza's claim of the autonomy of the attributes is an attack against the Cartesian primacy of thought, against the theoretical framework that effectively subsumes the body within the order of the mind, so too our Deleuzian claim of the autonomy of practice is a reaction to conceptions of a primacy of theory that effectively subsume practice within theory. For example, when we pose the question of a foundation or cause of a practical act, such as the 1917 Bolshevik insurrection, we cannot look to a theoretical reason that determined it, such as Marx's use of the dialectic in *Capital*, but instead we must search for an accumulation of desires, imaginations, and powers that coincide and become necessary in the event; we need to search, in other words, for the common notions that transformed the joyful passions of the revolutionary encounter into actions. Once again, this proposition of the relative autonomy of a constitutive practice should be read as a polemical position, as an attempt to bring practice out from the shadow of theory and recognize its full force. Just as Spinoza said of the body, Deleuze might say, no one has yet determined what practice can do. The articulation of the practical function of the common notion in Spinoza, however, is a large step toward discovering the power of social practice.

Finally, in contrast to Deleuze, Althusser remains too Hegelian in the continual reemergence of the priority of theory and the continual subsumption of practice within the theoretical domain. The central project of materialist philosophy, in its many historical guises, is precisely to combat this proposition of priority, to challenge the notion of interrelation as subsumption: Bring the body out from the shadow of the mind, bring practice out from the shadow of theory, in all its autonomy and dignity, to try to discover what it can do. With his conception of a practice of common notions, a materialist practice of constitution that refuses to be recuperated within the movement of theory, Deleuze has completely removed himself from the Hegelian terrain. This practical practice cannot be subsumed within the unfolding of spirit in its progressive instantiations. The logic of constitution reveals a progression that marches to a different beat, that accumulates its elements from below in open, nonteleological forms as original, unforeseeable, creative structures. The movement of a Hegelian practice is always recuperated within the logic of order, dictated from above, whereas a Deleuzian practice rises from below through an open logic of organization.

3.10 The Art of Organization: Toward a Political Assemblage

Politics arises in Spinoza as a question of bodies. "In order to really think
in terms of power, one must pose the question in relation to the body"
(*Expressionism in Philosophy: Spinoza* 257). The introduction of the ontological principle of power was the key that opened the field of Spinozian
practice for Deleuze, and the question of the power of the body served as
its primary terrain, as its model. We have seen that Deleuze's interpretation
of the common notions in terms of the logic of assemblage has brought to
light the real constitutive force of Spinozian practice: A passive affection
constitutes an active affection, imagination constitutes reason. The common notion is an ontological mechanism that forges being out of becoming, necessity out of chance. It is the ontological assemblage whereby the
chance joyful encounter is made adequate; the joyful encounter returns.
From the beginning, Deleuze has posed the common notion and its process of assemblage as part of an ethical project (becoming active, becoming adequate, becoming joyful), but how can we recognize this process in
properly political terms? What is the Spinozian process of political constitution, or rather, what is a political assemblage?

Spinoza is able to pose political questions directly in ontological terms
by constructing a passage through the juridical domain. The theory of
power and bodies is brought closer to political practice in the form of a
theory of right: "All that a body can do (its power), is also its 'natural
right' " (257). Spinoza's theory of natural right, along with that of Hobbes,
is greatly different from the natural law of the ancients. The ancients defined natural law in terms of perfection; they conceived of nature as oriented toward its ends, toward a final cause. Spinoza, as we have seen on
several occasions, always rejects the final cause for the efficient cause: "The
law of nature is no longer referred to a final perfection but to the initial
desire, to the strongest 'appetite' " (259). To understand this proposition of
natural right we have to recognize that Spinoza's ontological logic of assemblage and constitution guides the reasoning here: organization versus
order. The productivity of being itself is the motor that animates the entire
discourse on right. Let us take a moment to work through this constitutive
procedure, which should by now be very familiar.

We start with a devalorization. Just as we have seen on other terrains,
Spinoza insists that we begin our political thought from the lowest level of
our power, from the lowest point of social organization, with a typically
Machiavellian *ritorno ai principi*. Just as no one is born rational, so too no
one is born citizen. Since no order is predetermined, every element of
Spinozian society must be constituted internally with the elements at hand,
by the constituent subjects (be they ignorant or learned), on the basis of

the existing affections (be they passions or actions). And we know that the human condition is characterized predominantly by our weakness, that our power to be affected is filled largely by passions. This devalorization, however, is also an affirmation of our freedom. When Spinoza insists that our natural right is coextensive with our power, this means that no social order can be imposed by any transcendent elements, anything outside of the immanent field of forces, and thus any conception of duty or morality must be secondary and dependent on the assertion of our power. "True natural laws are norms of power, not rules of duty" (268). The expression of power free from any moral order is the primary ethical principle of society. "Pushing to the utmost what one can do [aller jusqu'au bout de ce qu'on peut] is the properly ethical task. It is here that the *Ethics* takes the body as model; for every body extends its power as far as it can. In a sense every being, each moment, pushes to the utmost what it can do" (269). This ethical formulation does not primarily place the accent on the limitation (*le bout*) of our power, but rather it poses a dynamic between the limit and what we can do—each time we reach an extreme point, what we can do rises up to move beyond. The ethical task highlights our perseverance, our material *conatus* moving in the world to express our power beyond the given limits of the present arrangement, the present order. This ethical perseverance is the open expression of multiplicity. Spinoza's conception of natural right, then, poses the freedom from order, the freedom of multiplicity, the freedom of society in anarchy.

The society described by the state of nature itself, however, presents us with an unlivable condition, or, more accurately, it presents us with the minimum point of our power. In the state of nature thus conceived, I experience chance encounters with other bodies that, since we are predominantly determined by passions, have very little in common with my own. Therefore, in this condition, not only is my power to be affected filled predominantly by passive affections, but also those passive affections are mostly sad. Just as previously we have moved from passive affections to active affections and from imagination to reason, here we must discover a passage for the increase of our power from natural right to civil right. "There could be only one way to make the state of nature livable: by striving to *organize its encounters*" (260-61). The civil state is the state of nature made livable; or, more precisely, it is the state of nature infused with the project of the increase of our power. And, as we have seen, the increase of our power involves the organization of composable relationships: "If two come together and unite their strength, they have jointly more power, and consequently more right over nature, than either of them alone; and the more there be that join in alliance, the more right they will collectively possess" (*Political Treatise* II:13). The heart of Spinozian politics, then, is oriented toward the organization of social encounters so as to encourage useful and composable relationships; it is "this art of organizing encounters" (262). Natural right is not negated in the passage to civil right, as it is in dialectical conceptions of society, but rather it is preserved and intensified, just as imagination is fortified in reason. In this transformation the multiplicity of society is forged into a multitude.[20] The multitude remains contingent in that it is always open to antagonism and conflict, but in its dynamic of increasing power it attains a plane of consistency; it has the capacity to pose social normativity as civil right. The multitude is multiplicity made powerful. Spinoza's conception of civil right, then, complements the first notion of freedom with a second: from the freedom from order to the freedom of organization; the freedom of multiplicity becomes the freedom of the multitude. And the rule of the multitude is democracy: "This right, which is defined by the power of the multitude, is generally called a State. And it is absolutely controlled by he who through common consent manages the affairs of the republic. . . . If this charge belongs to a council composed of the general multitude, then the State is called a democracy" (*Political Treatise* II:17). In the passage of freedom, then, from multiplicity to multitude, Spinoza composes and intensifies anarchy in democracy. Spinozian democracy, the absolute rule of the multitude through the equality of its constituent members, is founded on the "art of organizing encounters" (262).

This vision of the freedom and organization of social encounters is, in effect, an extension of Deleuze's ontological theory of common notions. On the epistemological plane, we have seen how the common notion is the mechanism by which practice constitutes an order of knowledge; the practical passage from the joyful passive affection to the active affection, just like the passage from imagination to reason, develops through the common notion. Now, the theory of ontological parallelism tells us that if we can identify such a practical passage in the realm of thought, we must be able to recognize a similar passage in the realm of extension. In other words, if we are to pursue Deleuze's interpretation of parallelism consistently, we have to discover a corporeal common notion that serves to organize the chance, inadequate, and predominantly sad encounters of social bodies into coherent, adequate, and joyful encounters, just as on the basis of inadequate ideas (imagination) the intellectual common notion constitutes adequate ideas (reason). Pushed to its conceptual limits, ontological parallelism means that the constitution of knowledge, the intellectual constitution of community, must be equalled and complemented by a corporeal constitution of community. The corporeal common notion, the adequate social body, is given material form in the multitude.

These outlines of Spinozian freedom and democracy provide us with a general political orientation, but the central element, the process of the formation of the multitude, the process of political assemblage, risks appearing obscure and mysterious until we flesh out its concrete constitutive mechanisms. This, however, is the limit of Deleuze's analysis in *Expressionism in Philosophy: Spinoza*. In effect, this is the limit of a "theory" of democracy, the point at which theory runs into a wall. Only social practice can break through this wall, by giving body to the process of political assemblage.

Chapter 4

Conclusion
An Apprenticeship in Philosophy

We have navigated through Deleuze's early work to discern a powerful line of development, a progressive evolution: Bergson, Nietzsche, Spinoza. This is not, however, merely an exercise in the history of philosophy. It is true that part of my interest in this study has been to demonstrate through Deleuze's work that the history of metaphysics is not dead, that it contains powerful and radical alternatives still very alive in the contemporary problems we face. These philosophers form a foundation for Deleuze's thought in that they provide the material for his own education, for his apprenticeship in philosophy. Deleuze's work, however, does not stop with a revalorization of this alternative tradition: He selects what is living and transforms it, making it adequate to his concerns. In this way, he both makes the history of philosophy his own and makes it new.

Today, an emerging generation is being schooled in Deleuze's thought, developing a new taste for philosophy. In this study I have tried to read Deleuze's work using his method of selection and transformation in order to pursue my own education, my own apprenticeship in philosophy. I have tried to make his work my own. In the process, I have fleshed out a cluster of four themes that coalesce in my mind as the core of this endeavor: ontology, affirmation, practice, and constitution.

4.1 Ontology

Deleuze's ontology is grounded in the conceptions of difference and singularity that he discovers in Bergson and Spinoza. Bergsonian difference defines, above all, the principle of the positive *movement* of being, that is, the temporal principle of ontological articulation and differentiation. Bergson does not ask what being is, but how it moves. This focus on ontological movement can easily be situated in the context of traditional philosophical discussions on the nature of causality. Bergsonian difference must first be distinguished from the difference of the Mechanicists, who pose an empirical evolution in which each determination is caused by a material "other" through an accidental relation. The ontological movement of the Mechanicists rests on a crude conception of the material cause that risks posing being as purely contingent, as a "subsistent exteriority." On the other hand, however, Bergsonian difference must be distinguished from Platonic difference, which relies not on a material cause, but a final cause. The Platonic ontological movement is equally external in that it is determined by its end, by its finality. Finally, Bergsonian difference must be distinguished above all from Hegelian difference, which rests on an "abstract" conception of causality: abstract in the sense that the negative movement of contradictions poses a cause that is absolutely external to its effect. Opposition, Deleuze claims, is too crude a notion to capture the nuances that mark real differences; it hangs loosely on reality like baggy clothes. Bergson's difference, in contrast to all these versions, is defined by a notion of efficient causality. The movement of being is a progression of internal differences in that the cause always inheres within its effect. In this way, ontological movement is freed from any play of negations and is posed instead as absolutely positive, as an internal differentiation.

In the Spinozian context, the positivity of being is characterized by its singularity and its univocal expression. The singularity of Spinoza's being is not defined by its difference from an other, from nonbeing, but rather by the fact that being is different in itself. "Dissociated from any numerical distinction, real distinction is carried into the absolute. It becomes capable of expressing the difference in being and consequently it brings about the restructuring of other distinctions" (*Expressionism in Philosophy: Spinoza* 39). Spinozian being is remarkable; it is different without any external reference. In other words, being is singular. Once again, this logic points to the tradition of causal arguments. Just as being is cause of itself and thus supported by an internal causal structure, so too being is different in itself and thus sustained through a notion of internal or efficient difference. The expression of this internal difference is precisely the movement of being. Expression is the opening of being that makes clear its internal causal structure, its genealogy, and thus the expression of singular being cannot but be univocal: Being is expressed always and everywhere *in the same voice*. The singular and univocal expression of being is, in the Spinozian context, the highest possible affirmation of being. And this proposition casts our thought on the highest plane of ontological speculation.

There should be no doubt at this point that this Deleuzian conception of ontology is radically distinct from the Hegelian and Heideggerian conceptions, particularly with regard to its positivity and its materialism. In Spinozian shorthand, we could say that Deleuze has displaced the center of ontological speculation from "omnis determinatio est negatio" to "non opposita sed diversa"—from negation to difference. This strategy strikes at the very first moves of Hegel's logic, the progression from pure being to determinate being, and, more important, it strikes at the movement of the entire dialectical system. In essence, Deleuze appeals to the precritical world of Spinoza and the Scholastics to demonstrate the weakness of Hegelian ontology. The being that must seek an external support for its difference, the being that must look to negation for its foundation, is no being at all. As we know from Scholastic arguments about the "productivity" and "producibility" of being—its aptitudes to produce and to be produced—a thing cannot be the necessary cause of something outside itself, and an effect cannot have more perfection or reality than its cause. (See Etienne Gilson, *La philosophie au Moyen Age* 595.) The dignity of being is precisely its power, its internal production—that is, the efficient causal genealogy that rises from within, the positive difference that marks its singularity. Real being is singular and univocal; it is different in itself. From this efficient difference at the heart of being flows the real multiplicity of the world. In comparison, Hegelian being can manage neither a real unity nor a real multiplicity—it is abstract in the sense that it can grasp neither its power to produce nor its power to be produced.

Only materialism can adequately grasp this understanding of being. Materialism must be understood here as a polemical position that combats any priority afforded to thought over matter, to mind over body, not in order to invert that relationship and give matter the same privilege, but rather to establish an equality between the two realms. Deleuze's ontology requires a materialist perspective because any priority accorded to thought would weaken the internal structure of being. Materialism, then, is not only a refusal of the subordination of the corporeal to the mental world, but also an exaltation of being with respect to both realms. Deleuze refuses any idealistic conception that in some way subordinates being to thought. "The being of Hegelian logic," for example, "is merely 'thought' being, pure and empty" (*Nietzsche and Philosophy* 183). Deleuze's being is logically prior to, and comprehensive of, thought and extension equally. This logical priority, however, does not mean that being exists at a distance from the actual world; there is no separation between being and nature. Any term such as being-in-the-world would have no sense in Deleuze's ontology because being is always already actual; it is always fully expressed in body and thought. Only a materialist approach can adequately account for both this superficiality and this plenitude.

A first lesson we can draw from Deleuze's philosophy, then, is that what some suppose to be the masterline of metaphysical speculation—from Plato to Hegel and Heidegger—does not have a monopoly on ontological thought. He brings out the coherence of an alternative tradition—from Lucretius and Duns Scotus to Spinoza and Bergson—that is equally rich and varied. In effect, to contest the claims of an idealist ontology we do not need to go all the way to the opposite and propose a deontological perspective, but rather we can pursue the materialist ontological tradition as an alternative. One of the advantages of choosing this alternative is that it allows us to bring out the productivity and producibility of nature, and hence our power to act and our power to be affected. A positive, materialist ontology is above all an ontology of power.

4.2 Affirmation

Like the notion of positive ontology, so too the concept of affirmation has been misunderstood and ridiculed by the Hegelian tradition. The great thinkers of the Frankfurt School, for example, have conceived of affirmation as a passive acceptance of the contemporary state of affairs, as a naive and irresponsible optimism. (See, for example, Herbert Marcuse, *Reason and Revolution* viiff.) Contemporary Hegelians continue this vein of criticism when they claim that philosophies of affirmation remain impotent because they have deprived themselves of the power of negation, they have lost the "magic" of the labor of the negative (Judith Butler, *Subjects of Desire* 183-84; see also my "La renaissance hégélienne américaine et l'intériorisation du conflit" 134-38). Affirmation is thus conceived as uncritical, or even anticritical, thinking. Here we are once again faced with a nuance or an alternative that is misunderstood as a polar opposition. In other words, Deleuzian affirmation does indeed contest the Hegelian form of negation and critique, but it does not reject negation and critique *tout court*; rather it highlights the nuances that form alternative conceptions of negation and critique more adequate to his project.

Affirmation, then, is not opposed to critique. On the contrary, it is based on a total, thoroughgoing critique that pushes the forces of negation to their limit. Affirmation is intimately tied to antagonism. The form of the Deleuzian critique harks back to the Scholastic philosophical method: *pars destruens, pars construens*. The key to this alternative conception is the absolute, nondialectical character of the negative moment. This is the way in which Nietzsche "completes" the Kantian project, according to Deleuze.

The Kantian critique must remain partial and incomplete because it guards the suprasensible as a privileged terrain, protecting it from the destructive forces of the critique: Kant can treat claims to truth and morality without endangering truth and morality themselves. The transcendental reserve shields the essential order from any radical destruction or restructuring. Nietzsche wants to give the critical forces free reign, to unleash them across the unlimited horizon so that all values of the established order would be at risk. "One of the principal motifs of Nietzsche's work is that Kant had not carried out a true critique because he was not able to pose the problem of critique in terms of values" (*Nietzsche and Philosophy* 1). The total critique is always insurrectional; it is an unrestrained attack on the established values and the ruling powers they support; it is a *mise en cause* of the entire contemporary horizon. The negation that forms the core of the total critique is nondialectical precisely because it refuses the conservative attitude of the dialectic: It does not recuperate the essence of its enemy, it does not "preserve and maintain what is superseded" (*Phenomenology of Spirit* §188). There is thus no magical resurrection of the other within the same, but rather a pure and uncompromising antagonism. This is not to say that all that is present is negated, but simply that what is negated is attacked with unrestrained force.

Deleuze's affirmative philosophy does not refuse or ignore the power of the negative, then, but rather points toward a different concept of negation—a negation that opens the field of affirmation. The destruction without reserve creates the space for free and original creative forces. The slave logic of the dialectic tries to pull an affirmation out of the supersession of the negation, but in this case the affirmation is already prefigured in the negation—it is merely a repetition of the same. The master logic, in contrast, engenders a true affirmation that stands on a separate footing. In itself, this negation involves no preservation, but rather a real rupture, a transmutation. The subsequent affirmation, then, looks only to its own power. The love of Ariadne for Dionysus is perhaps the ultimate expression of this affirmation in Nietzsche's work. Dionysus is the god of affirmation, but only Ariadne can affirm affirmation itself: "Eternal affirmation of being, eternally I am your affirmation" (*Nietzsche and Philosophy* 187). Ariadne's affirmation is a double affirmation, the affirmation of affirmation itself, "the 'yes' that responds to 'yes'" ("Mystère d'Ariane" 151). This is a spiraling affirmation that feeds on its own power, the affirmation that returns: affirmation raised to the *n*th power. Ariadne's affirmation of being is an ethical act, an act of love.

It should be clear that this Deleuzian affirmation is not a mere acceptance of what is. The yes of the ass, the yes of the one who does not know how to say no, is merely the caricature of affirmation. On the contrary, only

the one who knows how to wield a powerful negation can pose a real affirmation. The no of the total critique, the expression of an unrestrained
negation, is liberating—it makes one lighter. "To affirm is not to take re-
sponsibility for, to take on the burden of what is, but to release, to set free
what lives. To affirm is to unburden: not to load life with the weight of
higher values, but to create new values which are those of life, which make
life light and active" (*Nietzsche and Philosophy* 185). Affirmation is not the
acceptance of being; Deleuze would have it instead that affirmation is actually the creation of being. The concept of affirmation allows Deleuze to
transport the power of his ontology to the terrain of sense and value, and
thus to formulate an ethics of being. Ethics here is precisely a line of conduct, or a practical guide, for the expression of power, for the active production of being.

4.3 Practice

Affirmation, however, is not enough for a Deleuzian ethics. An ethical
project cannot remain on the plane of speculation, but must find an avenue
to enter the field of practice. Spinoza's conception of joy gives Deleuze the
key to this new terrain: "The sense of joy appears as the properly ethical
sense; it is to practice what affirmation itself is to speculation. . . . A philosophy of pure affirmation, the *Ethics* is also a philosophy of the joy corresponding to such affirmation" (*Expressionism in Philosophy: Spinoza* 272).
The affirmation of speculation, then, must be complemented by the joy of
practice. This is how ethics realizes its full constructive force, as a practical
constitution of being. In effect, affirmative speculation needs a corresponding joyful practice to make good on its claims to creativity and activity. Affirmation by itself, in other words, risks appearing as simply that which
grasps and selects the being that is; joy is properly the moment that creates
the being to come.

Much of Deleuze's work is concerned with the problem of practice:
How can we set the creative forces in motion? How can we make philosophy truly practical? Deleuze finds the key in the investigation of power. The
mobile and malleable conception of being found in Bergson and Spinoza
already prepares the terrain for this work: Deleuze's ontology focuses on
the movement of being, on its genealogy of causal relations, on its "productivity" and "producibility." The thematic of power and production,
then, already occupies an essential position. In Nietzsche, Deleuze dis-
cerns a distinction between two qualities of power, the active and the reactive, that is, power linked to what it can do and power separated from
what it can do. In Spinoza, this same distinction is given a richer definition
with respect to the adequate and the inadequate: The adequate is that

which expresses (or envelops or comprehends) its cause; the inadequate is mute. Like the active, the adequate is linked forward to what it can do; but it is also linked backward to its internal genealogy of affects, the genealogy of its own production. The adequate gives full view to both the productivity and the producibility of being. This is the crucial relation that opens up the field of power for Deleuze: Corresponding to the power of being to act and exist is its power to be affected. This power of producibility provides the communicating corridor between ontology and practice.

The importance of the power to be affected is that it reveals distinctions within our power; the power to act and exist, in contrast, appears as pure spontaneity, undifferentiated, and thus remains opaque to our analysis. We must delve, then, into the distinctions within power, within our affectivity, in order to discover the point of departure for an ethical practice. Deleuze's investigation of our power to be affected reveals two tiers of distinctions: At the first level, he poses the distinction between active affections and passive affections; and at the second, he poses the distinction between joyful passive affections and sad passive affections. As Deleuze formulates each of these distinctions within our power, he also recognizes that the human condition lies principally on the weak side of the equation: Our power to be affected is dominated by passive rather than active affections, and the majority of our passive affections are sad rather than joyful. This Spinozian "pessimism" is precisely the point of departure for a joyful practice. With this realistic assessment of our condition, we are ready to set out on the steep path to increase our power, to become joyful, to become active.

Deleuze begins the elaboration of practice on the field of chance encounters and focuses on the encounters with bodies that agree with our nature, that increase our power: encounters that engender joyful passions. A joyful passion, since it is a passion, is always the result of an external cause, and thus always indicates an inadequate idea; however, since it is joyful, it nonetheless opens an avenue toward adequacy: "We must then, *by the aid of joyful passions*, form the idea of what is common to some external body and our own. For this idea alone, this common notion, is adequate" (*Expressionism in Philosophy: Spinoza* 283). Joyful passions are the precondition for practice; they are the raw material for the construction of the common notion. In effect, the common notion is already latent in the joyful passion, because joy necessarily results from an encounter with a body that has a relationship that is compatible or composable with our own. The joy of the encounter is precisely the composition of the two bodies in a new, more powerful body. When our mind forms an idea of the common relationship shared between this body and our body (a common notion), the joyful affection ceases to be passive and becomes active. The construction of the common notion is, in effect, the enveloping or comprehension of the cause of the affection, and an affection that expresses its cause is no longer passive, but active. The joy of the active affection is no longer contingent on a chance encounter; the joy supported by the common notion is the joy that returns. This is the practical process that fleshes out Deleuze's ethical mandates: Become joyful, become active.

Joyful practice brings ethics back to ontology—it exploits the producibility or composability of being. This is perhaps the largest payoff for Deleuze's extensive and complex investigation into ontology. Being is a hybrid structure constituted through joyful practice. When the common notion envelops the cause of a joyful encounter, and thus makes that encounter adequate, it is making a new incision into being, constructing a new assemblage of its structure. What raises this encounter to the level of being is precisely its comprehension of the cause: Substance, as Spinoza tells us, is that which is cause of itself. The practice of joy is the construction of ontological assemblages, and thus the active constitution of being.

4.4 Constitution

Many American authors have tried to pose the general question of the political consequences of poststructuralism. Such investigations have led to a wide range of judgments across the political spectrum. Indeed, one should not expect to find a clear response to such a question about a broad theoretical movement. For example, during the past 150 years, Hegel's philosophy has served as a primary support for a wide variety of political positions, both regressive and progressive, many of which have differed greatly from Hegel's own political views. One should not, of course, look for *the* political position that follows necessary from a theoretical body of work. There is not one, but many corridors one can follow for the passage to action. It will not be very fruitful, then, to attempt a general definition of the politics of poststructuralism, or even of the politics of Deleuze's philosophy. It is more appropriate and more productive to ask ourselves, What can Deleuze's thought afford us? What can we make of Deleuze? In other words, what are the useful tools we find in his philosophy for furthering our own political endeavors? In this spirit, I have tried to discover in Deleuze some tools for the constitution of a radical democracy. The distinctions that I have tried to highlight in Deleuze's work pose the multiplicity of organization against the multiplicity of order, and the assemblages of power (*les agencements de la puissance*) against the deployments of power (*les dispositifs du pouvoir*). Each of these distinctions hinges on a notion of constitution that remains latent, but nonetheless central, in Deleuze's thought. From this perspective, Deleuze can help us develop a dynamic conception of democratic society as open, horizontal, and collective.

To an extent, this vision of democracy coincides with that of liberalism. Perhaps the most important single tenet of liberal democratic theory is that the ends of society be indeterminate, and thus that the movement of society remain open to the will of its constituent members. The priority of right over good is thought to insure that the freedom of society's development is not constricted or closed by an externally determined *telos*. This political refusal of teleology leads directly to a philosophical refusal of ontology, because ontology itself is presumed to carry with it a transcendental determination of the good. Deontology, then, is the only philosophical position that can support a democratic society open to a multiplicity of ends. Liberal thinkers who reason in this fashion have, in effect, too quickly accepted the Platonic and Hegelian claims about the link between ontology and social teleology; they are still too tied to the logic of contradictions, and thus they miss the important nuances. In other words, in opposition to an ontological vision that determines a conservative, closed society, they believe that a deontological theory is necessary to allow for a democratic, open society. One need not, however, make this leap to the opposite pole, one need not reject ontology *tout court*, in order to affirm the openness of ends in society. The tradition of Western metaphysics is not of a piece, it is not a monolithic block, but rather contains within itself radical alternatives. (The fact that the tradition appears to some so thin in alternatives is really only evidence of the weak state of contemporary philosophical inquiry.) When Deleuze interrogates Bergson, Nietzsche, and Spinoza, in fact, he is reaffirming and articulating an alternative tradition within the history of Western metaphysics that presents a strong notion of ontology but does not propose any teleological mapping or any determination of ends. What Deleuze develops coincides with the liberal vision in its affirmation of the openness of ends in democratic society, but it does not for that reason refuse the tradition of ontological discourse. Deleuzian being is open to the intervention of political creations and social becomings: This openness is precisely the "producibility" of being that Deleuze has appropriated from Scholastic thought. The power of society, to translate in Spinozian terms, corresponds to its power to be affected. The priority of the right or the good does not enter into this conception of openness. What is open, and what links the ontological to the political, is the expression of power: the free conflict and composition of the field of social forces.

This open organization of society must be distinguished from the vertical structures of order. By organization here I do not understand any sort of plan or blueprint of how social relationships will be structured; on the contrary, by organization I understand a continual process of composition and decomposition through social encounters on an immanent field of forces. The skyline of society is perfectly flat, perfectly horizontal, in the sense that social organization proceeds without any predetermined design, on the basis of the interaction of immanent forces, and can thus, in principle, be thrust back at any time, as if by the indefatigable pressures of gravity, to its zero state of equality. Organization carries within itself the destructive power of Machiavelli's *ritorno ai principi*. This is not to say that social institutions (or other instances of verticality) are not formed, but that they receive a strictly immanent determination, and thus remain always and completely susceptible to restructuring, reform, and destruction (in the spirit, for example, of the Communards, who insisted that all representation be subject to immediate revocation). *Dispositifs*, or deployments, structure a social order from above, from an external space of transcendence; *agencements*, or assemblages, constitute the mechanisms of social organization from below, from the immanent social plane. The horizontality of the material constitution of society puts the weight on practice as the motor of social creation. A practical politics of social bodies sets loose the immanent forces from the strictures of predetermined forms to discover their own ends, invent their own constitution. Once again, we find that the productivity of social being corresponds to its producibility. The horizontal society is the open site that fosters practical creation and composition as well as destruction and decomposition. The model of this constitution is the general assembly, the absolute and equal inclusion of the entire immanent plane: Democracy, as Spinoza is fond of saying, is the absolute form of government.

The processes of social assemblage, of social constitution, are indifferent to the boundaries posed by individualism; or, more precisely, the borders of social bodies are continually subject to change as the practice of assemblage decomposes certain relationships and composes others. There is no contradiction, then, between the individual and the collective; the constitution of society rests on a different axis. The process of political assemblage, the composition of joyful social relationships, moves instead between multiplicity and the multitude. The Deleuzian practice of affirmation and joy, in other words, is directed toward creating social bodies or planes of composition that are ever more powerful, while they remain at the same time open to internal antagonisms, to the real forces of destruction and decomposition. Political assemblage is certainly an art in that it has to be continually made anew, continually reinvented. The multitude is assembled through this practice as a social body defined by a common set of behaviors, needs, and desires. This is Deleuze's way of grasping the living force in society that continually emerges from the dead forces of social order, just like Marx's living labor that refuses to be sucked dry by the vampires set in flight by capital. And this quality of living is defined both by the power to act and the power to be affected: a social body without organs. The composition or the constitution of the multitude does not in any way negate the multiplicity of social forces, but on the contrary, raises the multiplicity to a higher level of power.

All of this, however, remains only the hint of a democratic politics; we still have to flesh out its constitutive mechanisms with concrete social practices. What Deleuze gives us, in effect, is a general orientation that can suggest the paths of future research into the contemporary forms of social assemblage. On the political horizon, the multiplicity of social practices and desires presents us with the conditions of composition or assemblage. This is the field on which the process must be defined: Assemblage must be pursued by bringing together social bodies with compatible internal relationships, with composable practices and desires. In the existing social practices, in the affective expressions of popular culture, in the networks of laboring cooperation, we should seek to discern the material mechanisms of social aggregation that can constitute adequate, affirmative, joyful relationships and thus powerful subjective assemblages. Filling out the passage from multiplicity to multitude remains for us the central project for a democratic political practice.

Notes

Introduction

1. This is the argument, for example, of Stephen Houlgate in *Hegel, Nietzsche and the Criticism of Metaphysics*. We will return to his arguments to consider them carefully in chapter 2, "Remark: The Resurgence of Negativity."

2. In addition to Judith Butler's *Subjects of Desire* and Stephen Houlgate's *Hegel, Nietzsche and the Criticism of Metaphysics*, see Gillian Rose, *Dialectic of Nihilism*, and John Grumley, *History and Totality: Radical Historicism from Hegel to Foucault*. For an account that does recognize a successful rupture from the Hegelian problematic in the French thought of the 1960s, see Michael Roth, *Knowing and History: Appropriations of Hegel in Twentieth-Century France*.

3. We will deal with the refusal of an "intellectualist" account of being and the bases of a materialist ontology at length in terms of Deleuze's interpretation of the attributes in Spinoza (see Sections 3.4 and 3.5). I do not directly confront Deleuze's ontology with that of Heidegger, but I think posing this question could be very fruitful and deserves a complete study of its own. Here I hope only to indicate the general lines of confrontation so as to offer a helpful guidepost and situate Deleuze's approach.

4. Some authors have recently begun to use "foundation" and "foundationalism" to refer to an idealist conception of the necessary and eternal bedrock that underlies and determines the unfolding of epistemological, ontological, and ultimately ethical developments and "grounding" to refer to a materialist and historical conception of the humus or, more appropriately, the geological sediment that forms the context of our contemporary interventions. Although this is similar to the conceptual distinction I am referring to, I have reservations about the appropriateness of the terms "foundation" and "ground." The organic metaphors evoked by "ground" carry all the problems of a predetermined, "natural" structure or order. (See, for example, Deleuze and Guattari's critique of root structures in "Introduction: Rhizome," *A Thousand Plateaus*.) Furthermore, in the specific context of our study, ground

(*Grund*) plays such a central role in the Hegelian system (see, for example, *Science of Logic* 444-78) that it is difficult to recuperate any difference it might mark from foundation.

Preliminary Remark

1. I do not mean to suggest that Deleuze's book on Hume is in some way incidental. I have chosen to take a certain slice across the body of Deleuze's work that I have found particularly productive, but it is by no means the only way to approach his work. I have simply done my best to make Deleuze's work my own.

2. Brian Massumi, to my mind the best reader of Deleuze, provides us with a pertinent example. In his Foreword to *A Thousand Plateaus*, Massumi is certainly correct to insist on Deleuze's opposition to "State philosophy." However, Massumi (and admittedly Deleuze too at times) tends to exaggerate the centrality and hegemony of "State philosophy" in the history of Western thought: " 'State philosophy' is another word for the representational thinking that has characterized Western metaphysics since Plato" (xi). Western metaphysics should not be characterized in such a univocal manner; the philosophical tradition contains radical alternatives within it. As a result of this simplification, we also find the tendency to exaggerate the marginality of the opposing tradition that is dear to Deleuze; in other words, even if Lucretius, Duns Scotus, Spinoza, et al. form a "minority" in the sense that they are partially eclipsed by the contemporary political-academic hegemony of "State philosophy" (Plato, Hegel, etc.), nonetheless this "minority" constitutes some of the highest and most central moments of Western metaphysics. My point is that we should not minimize the coherence and the enormous power of this alternative tradition. In any case, Deleuze's opposition to "State philosophy" should not be conceived as an opposition to Western philosophy *tout court*, but rather as an affirmation of its most powerful and most lucid elements. It is perhaps because of this confusion that many in the United States mistakenly regard Deleuze as a "postmodern" thinker.

3. After Deleuze's presentation entitled "La méthode de dramatisation" (The method of dramatization) before the Société française de philosophie, Deleuze's respected professor Ferdinand Alquié charged that by exclusively drawing on examples from biology, psychology, and other fields Deleuze had lost the understanding of the specificity of properly philosophical discourse. Deleuze was noticeably hurt by this accusation and he gave an emotional, affectionate response: "Your other reproach touches me even more. Because I believe entirely in the specificity of philosophy and I owe this conviction to you yourself" (106). What Alquié seemed to misunderstand is that although Deleuze's exemplification may be "unphilosophical," his reasoning and explanation are purely philosophical in the strictest sense.

4. We can see this point very clearly in Deleuze's relation to Duns Scotus: "There was never but one ontological proposition: Being is univocal. There was never but one ontology, that of Duns Scotus, who gave being one single voice. We say Duns Scotus because he knew how to raise univocal being to the highest point of subtlety, without giving in to abstraction" (*Différence et répétition* 52). From the point of view of the univocity of being, Deleuze sees the history of ontology as fundamentally supported by the arguments of Duns Scotus, Spinoza, and Nietzsche (52-61). The central point here, again, is that Deleuze is not pulling away from metaphysics, but on the contrary reaffirming its highest points.

5. Readers familiar with Deleuze's work might well question the order of my proposed evolution (Bergson-Nietzsche-Spinoza) because Deleuze's *Bergsonism* (1966) appeared after *Nietzsche and Philosophy* (1962). We can see in an early article, however, "La conception de la différence chez Bergson" (1956), that most of Deleuze's reading of Bergson was established well before he turned to Nietzsche. More important, we find that Deleuze's reading of Bergson leads logically to questions that he seeks to resolve in the study of Nietzsche; in turn, the

reading of Nietzsche reveals questions that lead him to study Spinoza. This is the trajectory I seek to trace from a logic of being to an ethics and finally a politics of being. Therefore, I would justify my proposition of an evolutionary sequence both on the basis of the historical order of Deleuze's consideration of the authors and the logical progression traced by his thought.

6. Even without close examination, the most general facts of Deleuze's biography, particularly the things that he did not do, indicate his difference from nearly all other major French philosophical voices to emerge from his generation: He was never a member of the French Communist Party, he did not attend the exclusive Ecole Normale Supérieure, and he was never fascinated by the work of Martin Heidegger.

Chapter 1. Bergsonian Ontology: The Positive Movement of Being

1. Hegel is apparently quoting here from *Letter 50* from Spinoza to Jarig Jelles. The original reads "Quia ergo figura non aliud, quàm determinatio, & determinatio negatio est; non poterit, ut dictum, aliud quid, quàm negatio, esse." That Hegel changes the quotation to simplify it for his purposes is not a serious issue; however, in his interpretation he completely distorts its Spinozian meaning. For an extensive analysis of Hegel's misreading of Spinoza's "negativism," see Pierre Macherey, *Hegel ou Spinoza*, pp. 141ff.

2. The work of the Scholastics (from Roger Bacon and Duns Scotus to William Ockham and, much later, Francisco Suárez) gives central ontological importance to causality and to the productivity of being. What I find most important in relation to Deleuze's work is the Scholastic mode of ontological reasoning and the criteria they establish for being. The power, necessity, perfection, reality, and univocity of being are all established through causal arguments; the divine essence is a productive capacity—it exists as the first cause, the efficient cause of everything. (Ockham adds that God is not only the efficient but also the immediate cause of everything.) As Etienne Gilson explains in relation to Duns Scotus, at the foundation of Scholastic ontology are the complementary properties of being: " 'causality' and 'producibility,' or the aptitudes to produce and to be produced" (*La philosophie au Moyen Age* 595). In the course of these ontological discussions, the Scholastics take meticulous care in elaborating and observing the principles of causality. Some of these principles will prove especially useful in our discussion: (1) an effect cannot have more perfection or reality than its cause; (2) a thing cannot be the necessary cause of something outside itself. Finally, while the efficient cause is primary in proofs of the existence of God, the Scholastics in general maintain the four genres of cause inherited from Aristotle (material, formal, efficient, and final) as real causes, even though they change the meaning of the genres significantly. For a detailed analysis of the genres of cause see Francisco Suárez, *Disputaciones metafísicas*, Disputación XII, Sección III.

3. It should come as no surprise, of course, that we find Scholastic resonances in Deleuze's study of Bergson, given both Deleuze's interest in the Scholastics (particularly Duns Scotus) and Bergson's extensive knowledge of Aristotle. Bergson wrote his Latin thesis on the concept of place in Aristotle.

4. In Spinoza we find two important modifications of this Scholastic relationship between being and causality: (1) God is not an uncaused first cause, but cause of itself, *causa sui*; (2) only efficient causes are accepted as real causes. Spinoza inherits the first change from Descartes, and Etienne Gilson explains clearly how this modification of Scholastic doctrine is not so much a departure as a refinement of Scholastic reasoning that serves to intensify the close relationship between causality and real being. "If everything has a cause, God has a cause; if God does not have a cause, one cannot say that everything has a cause, and consequently one cannot prove the existence of God by the principle of causality. This is why the Cartesian proof, instead of being the proof of a first cause that has no cause, is the proof of a

first cause that is cause of itself; for the Scholastic God of *pure action* he substitutes the God that is *causa sui* that will later be grasped by Spinoza" (*Discours de la méthode*, Gilson edition 327). The second modification that we find in Spinoza, the rejection of the formal and final causes, is directed against Descartes. See *Ethics* IP34-36 and IAppendix. (For an explanation of abbreviations in references to Spinoza's works, see chapter 3, note 4.

5. Duns Scotus defines a basic division between *causae per se* that are essentially ordered and *causae per accidens* that are accidentally ordered. See *Philosophical Writings*, p. 40.

6. Deleuze's discussion implicitly sets up a fundamental division in the philosophical tradition that appears historically as a progressively more radical antagonism between Platonism and Aristotelianism. On one side, Hegel inherits the errors of Platonic ontology and exaggerates them, taking them to their extreme. On the other side, the Scholastics and Bergson continually perfect the Aristotelian logic of being. The rough outline of the history of philosophy suggested here, then, has one axis from Plato to Hegel and another axis oriented in an altogether different direction from Aristotle to the Scholastics to Bergson.

7. It may seem at this point that the real antagonism between Bergson and Hegel resides not so much in the claims for the states of being (determinateness and difference), but in the processes that purport to achieve them (determination and differentiation). This line of reasoning could lead us to say that Bergson is adopting Hegel's ends but critiquing his means. However, this attempt to distinguish process from achieved state is a distortion of both Hegel and Bergson. As we noted earlier, in Hegel the state of determinateness is not only founded by a process of negation, but it is constituted by the continual movement of this dynamic. Similarly, Bergson's difference refers not to a static quidditas but to a continuous movement in time. Both Hegel and Bergson present philosophies of time in which no effective distinction can be made between state and process.

8. We will come back to this "explosive internal force that life carries within itself" because this notion is unclear at this point. Deleuze often invokes the Bergsonian intuition in this same context, but that concept does not clarify the situation for us. We should note at this point, however, that this obscure notion constitutes a central point in Bergson's system, as the dynamic of the articulation of being. It is precisely at this point that Nietzschean will to power and Spinozian *conatus* come into play in the later studies.

9. Hegel notes that in etymological terms determinate being (*Dasein*). means being-there, being in a certain place; but, Hegel continues, the idea of space here is irrelevant (*Science of Logic* 110). It is tempting to give significance to the German etymology and explain Deleuze's usage on this basis: Determinate being or *Dasein* relates to space and marks differences of degree, while the "indeterminate" being of differentiation relates to time and marks differences of nature. However, as we have already seen, Deleuze credits the Hegelian *Dasein* of the dialectic with neither differences of nature nor differences of degree: Hegelian being remains an abstraction.

10. This critique of the possible exists already in Deleuze's early period of Bergson study in the 1950s, although at this point he only makes a distinction between the possible and the virtual, not between the real and the actual ("Bergson" 288-89). The complete formulation comes in the second Bergson period, and it is repeated in exactly the same terms in "La méthode de dramatisation" (78-79) and in *Différence et répétition* (269-76). The critique of the possible is directed toward Descartes and takes a slightly different form in *Expressionism in Philosophy: Spinoza* (30-31, 38-39, 122-26). We will return to these passages later.

11. My point is certainly not to prove that Deleuze has derived his argument from the Scholastics. We can equally well attribute the Scholastic resonances to Bergson and his interest in Aristotle. What is important, however, is that we can understand this point in Deleuze's argument more clearly when we keep in mind the Scholastic arguments or ones with similar concerns.

12. Here we can finally make sense of Bergson's use of "determinate" and "indeterminate." Posed in a Hegelian context they have a completely different meaning. Yet the gap between these two terminological registers reveals a serious issue that has not been adequately treated. In one sense, Deleuze's being must be "determinate" in that being is necessary, qualified, singular, and actual. In the other sense, however, Deleuze's being must be "indeterminate" in that being is contingent and creative. Some of Deleuze's most cherished terms — such as unforeseeable (*imprévisible*), untimely (*intempestif*), and event (*événement*) — insist on this point.

13. The role of the formal distinction in Duns Scotus is to mediate the unity and the multiplicity, the universal and the individual, on two separate planes. See Gilson, *La philosophie au Moyen Age*, pp. 599ff. Deleuze will use the conception of the real distinction in Spinoza to critique the formal distinction of Duns Scotus in *Expressionism in Philosophy: Spinoza*, pp. 63-65.

14. At this point in his work Deleuze finds in Bergsonian *fabulation* only an explanation of obligation and the negation of human creativity. In some of his later works, particularly the books on cinema, he reinterprets "fable-making" or "confabulation" in a more positive light. In fact, in a recent interview with Antonio Negri, Deleuze suggests that we should go back to this Bergsonian concept to develop a notion of social constitution: "Utopia is not a good concept: there is rather a 'confabulation' common to people and to art. One ought to take up the Bergsonian notion of confabulation and give it a political meaning" ("Le devenir révolutionnaire et les créations politiques" 105).

15. It is precisely this final section of *Bergsonism* that irritated the French Bergson community. Later, in the "Remark," we will consider the review of Madeleine Barthélemy-Madaule in *Les études bergsoniennes* in which she focuses on this section and objects, "Bergson is not Nietzsche" (120). One might well ask of my reconstructed evolution of Deleuze's thought, Why does *Bergsonism* not fully incorporate the Nietzschean themes and go beyond them? A response would have to agree with Barthélemy-Madaule that Bergson is not Nietzsche; even though Deleuze's interpretative strategy involves a high degree of selectivity, he will never stretch one doctrine to conform to another.

16. A central passage in this regard is Deleuze's description of Callicles' attack on law in relation to Nietzsche: "Everything that separates a force from what it can do he calls law. Law, in this sense, expresses the triumph of the weak over the strong. Nietzsche adds: the triumph of reaction over action. Indeed, everything which separates a force is reactive as is the state of a force separated from what it can do. Every force which goes to the limit of its power is, on the contrary, active. It is not a law that every force goes to the limit, it is even the opposite of a law" (*Nietzsche and Philosophy* 58-59). This is how Nietzsche's conception of power can be read as a powerful antijuridicism. We will return to this passage later. For an explanation of the distinction between *jus* and *lex* in Spinoza, see Antonio Negri, *The Savage Anomaly*, pp. 96ff.

Chapter 2. Nietzschean Ethics: From Efficient Power to an Ethics of Affirmation

1. This is one example in which Deleuze appears a little overzealous in his attack on Hegel. "If one considers the ensemble of the history of philosophy, one would search in vain for a philosophy that could proceed by the question 'Qu'est-ce que?' . . . Maybe Hegel, maybe there is only Hegel, precisely because his dialectic, being a dialectic of the empty and abstract essence, is not separated from the movement of the contradiction" ("La méthode de dramatisation" 92). In the discussion following this presentation, Ferdinand Alquié chastised Deleuze on this account: "I regret the rejection, a bit too fast, of the question 'Qu'est-ce que?,'

and I cannot accept what you say, intimidating us a bit, at the beginning, that is, that no phi-losopher has posed this question, except Hegel" (104). Alquié argues, rightly I believe, that Hegel cannot be singled out so easily and that many philosophers (Plato, Leibniz, Kant, etc.) have emphasized the question "Qu'est-ce que?" in various degrees and in diverse contexts.

2. In this Nietzschean context, Deleuze presents the argument as if it were part of an attack on causality itself; but it is not difficult to bring this back to the notion of the internal cause developed earlier in the Bergson section. Indeed, the argument becomes clearer if we read it as an affirmation of internal cause rather than an attack on causality *tout court*. I would argue, further, that Nietzsche's entire polemic against causality could be read productively as a polemic against the external cause and an affirmation of the internal cause. For an example of Nietzsche's argument, see *Twilight of the Idols*, "The Four Great Errors," pp. 47-54.

3. With this polemical proposition of efficient power, Deleuze is participating in a long philosophical tradition. The ultimate source, perhaps, can be found in Aristotle's distinction between potential being and actual being in *Metaphysics*, Book 5. However, this argument can be found in various forms throughout the materialist tradition, from Ockham to Marx. In fact, Spinoza's distinction between *potestas* and *potentia*, which plays such a central role in Anto-nio Negri's reading, correlates very closely with Nietzsche's usage of slave power and master power. For an explanation of this distinction in Negri's interpretation of Spinoza, see my fore-word to *The Savage Anomaly*, "The Anatomy of power," pp. xi-xvi.

4. This evaluation of the two natures of power is one element that brings Deleuze's Nietz-sche very close to Spinoza: "By virtue and power [*potentia*] I mean the same thing" (*Ethics* IVD8).

5. Mario Tronti observes that precisely what is lacking in Hegel's master-slave dialectic is the question of value. This is why Marx needs to combine a critique of Hegel with a critique of Ricardo to arrive at his notion of labor value (*Operai e capitale* 133-43).

6. "There is certainly in the author a sort of resentment with respect to Hegelian philos-ophy that sometimes allows him to write penetrating passages, but sometimes, too, threatens to misguide him" ("Nietzsche et la philosophie" 353). Wahl is certainly correct in pointing to this danger. Deleuze's defense rests on his development of a nondialectical opposition, which would not be a *ressentiment*, but a pure aggression.

7. Kojève's reading is perhaps the purest version of a personalist interpretation of the confrontation between the master and the slave: "A human-individual comes face to face with a human-individual" (*Introduction to the Reading of Hegel* 10).

8. I can imagine an argument by which Hegel could be defended against the charge that slave contents are being attributed to essence here, but the reading of this passage as an af-firmation of labor as essence is so widespread in the Hegelian tradition that I think it is worth considering this point.

9. Nietzsche and Marx are united precisely on a Spinozian proposition: The essence of being is power (*Ethics* IP34). One might well object at this point that in my argument Nietz-sche and Marx are not attacking essence per se, but substituting one essence for another. This is true. I would maintain that just as Nietzsche's arguments against causality should be read as arguments against the external causality in favor of the internal cause, the attack on essence is the attack on an external form of essence. The will to power is the essence of being. In effect, charges of "essentialism" are defused in the context of both Marx and Nietzsche. It is true that each relies on a notion of essence, but in both cases it is a historical, material, living essence, a superficial essence that has nothing to do with the ideal, transcendental structures that are usually the issue of "essentialist" arguments.

10. The "refusal of work" was not only a slogan but also one of the central analytical cat-egories of Italian Marxism in the sixties and seventies. Just as Marx discovered surplus value as the general term that envelops the various forms of exploitation (rent, profit, etc.), the "re-

fusal of work" is the general term that comprehends the various forms of proletarian resistance, be it constructive or destructive, individual or collective: emigration, mass exodus, work stoppage, organized strikes, sabotage, and so on. We should be very clear, however, that the refusal of work is not the negation of productivity or creativity; rather, it is the refusal of a relationship of exploitation. In the terms of the tradition, it is the affirmation of proletarian productive force and the denial of capitalist relations of production.

11. In regards to the theme of the attack on essence and the joy of destruction, the connections between Nietzsche and Lenin are profound. For an explanation of Lenin's use of the phrase "the art of insurrection," see Antonio Negri, *La fabbrica della strategia*, pp. 68ff.

12. There is certainly a wide variety of differing accounts of what '68 was, and what it should have been. The reason I think that *Vogliamo tutto* best serves our purposes here is that it gives direct expression to the desires of the workers in action better than any other source I have found. In any case, even if I were to hold that this account is exemplary of the events of '68, I would not claim that it is representative. I should also point out that just as it is a particular reading of Nietzsche that we are following, one defined by Deleuze's selection, it is also a particular interpretation of Marx, that of Italian *operaismo* (workerism) as expressed by authors such as Mario Tronti and Antonio Negri. Deleuze finds resonances with the work of Tronti in his study of Foucault; see *Foucault*, p. 144, note 28 and p. 150, note 45.

13. Pierre Klossowski develops this idea of a selective ontology along different lines in his spectacular analysis, *Nietzsche et le cercle vicieux*. See, in particular, the chapter entitled "Le cercle vicieux en tant que doctrine sélective," pp. 177-249.

14. Jean Wahl admires Deleuze's formulation of the will to nothingness as the *ratio cognoscendi* of the will to power in general and the affirmation of the eternal return as its *ratio essendi*, but he finds it somewhat inappropriate for the Nietzschean context: "But isn't this exposé of Nietzsche's thought perhaps too Scholastic in appearance?" ("Nietzsche et la philosophie" 378). Wahl is certainly right to note that Deleuze is bringing in an element external to Nietzsche's thought, but, as I hope I have already shown, reference to the Scholastics can help bring to light the ontological grounding of Nietzsche's thought (in the analysis of power, of will, and of causality).

15. Hugh Tomlinson translates "pouvoir d'être affecté" as "capacity to be affected." "Capacity" is a very poor choice because the "pouvoir d'être affecté" does not imply any possibility, but rather is always actual.

16. I use "will," "appetite," and "desire" here according to their Spinozian definitions. Will is *conatus* with respect to the mind, and appetite is *conatus* with respect to the mind and the body. Desire is appetite together with consciousness of the appetite. See *Ethics* IIIP9S.

Chapter 3. Spinozian Practice: Affirmation and Joy

1. Although this work has had a much smaller general audience than Deleuze's other readings in the history of philosophy, his interpretation of Spinoza has revolutionized Spinoza studies. Along with the reading of Louis Althusser (developed by Pierre Macherey and Etienne Balibar), Deleuze's work is the major influence to have emerged in French Spinoza studies in the last thirty years. The French tradition is very rich. Aside from Deleuze and the Althusserians, some of the major twentieth-century figures who constitute this tradition are Ferdinand Alquié, Sylvain Zac, and Martial Gueroult. We will have ample opportunity to draw on their readings in the course of our study.

2. Nietzsche recognized that he had a spiritual companion in Spinoza. He wrote to his friend Franz Overbeck: "I am utterly amazed, utterly enchanted. I have a *precursor*, and what a precursor! I hardly knew Spinoza: that I should have turned to him just *now*, was inspired by 'instinct.' ... My lonesomeness, which, as on very high mountains, often made it hard for

me to breathe and made my blood rush out, is now at least a twosomeness" (Postcard to Overbeck, July 30, 1881, in *The Portable Nietzsche* 92).

3. In a letter to Léon Brunschvicg, Bergson wrote: "One could say that every philosopher has two philosophies: his own and that of Spinoza" (*Ecrits et paroles* 587). An acute analysis of the common themes in the two philosophers is presented by Sylvain Zac in "Les thèmes spinozistes dans la philosophie de Bergson." See also Rose-Marie Mossé-Bastide, "Bergson et Spinoza," which draws heavily on Bergson's courses at the Collège de France. The most significant theme that Deleuze chooses not to treat, both in Bergson and Spinoza, is that of religion and mysticism. Both Zac and Mossé-Bastide consider this a fundamental aspect of the Spinoza-Bergson relationship.

4. We will use the conventional abbreviated notation for referring to Spinoza's works. A stands for axiom, C for corollary, D for demonstration, Def for definition, P for proposition, and S for scholium. Roman numerals are used to refer to the five parts of the *Ethics*, and Arabic numerals to denote proposition or scholium numbers. Thus, *Ethics* IP8S2 refers to *Ethics*, Part I, proposition 8, scholium 2.

5. I use "difference" and "distinction" as if they were interchangeable here because they seem to fill the same role in Deleuze's thought. We might ask ourselves, however, if an important nuance could be discerned between the two terms. It may be, in fact, that the common usage of "difference" implies an other or external cause, and therefore, "distinction" would be a better term for defining the singularity of being. We should keep in mind, of course, the two separate contexts: Bergson's use of difference derives primarily from biology and Mechanicism, while consideration of distinctions in Spinoza must be linked first to Descartes, and then to the Scholastics.

6. Once we pose the common thesis of the singularity of being in Bergson and Spinoza, we have to acknowledge what is commonly held to be the important difference: "While Spinoza's philosophy is a philosophy of necessity, Bergson's philosophy is a philosophy of contingency" (Zac, "Les thèmes spinozistes" 126). Any student of the history of philosophy would point out, along with Zac, that Spinoza is an "absolute determinist," while Bergson constructs an ontology based on "unforeseeable newness." I am very suspicious, however, of this traditional opposition. In Deleuze's work, as in that of Spinoza, we find that the conventional distinctions between necessity and contingency, between determination and creativity, are effectively subverted.

7. Deleuze's insistence on the thematic of expression constitutes a polemic against semiology on ontological grounds. A system of signs does not recognize being as a productive dynamic; it does not help us understand being through its causal genealogy. The "absent cause," which supports much of the French structuralist and semiological discourse in the sixties, denies a positive ontological foundation. In contrast, a theory of expression seeks to make the cause present, to bring us back to an ontological foundation by making clear the genealogy of being.

8. On the relationship between Duns Scotus and Spinoza, Deleuze makes one of his rare forays into philosophical historiography (63-67). It is unlikely, he notes, that Spinoza would have read Duns Scotus directly; however, through Juan de Prado, who is certain to have read Duns Scotus, Spinoza could have received a Scotist account of univocity and the formal distinction. Deleuze then sets this axis of thought, Duns Scotus-Spinoza, against its enemy axis, Suárez-Descartes. The lines of battle are univocity, immanence, and expression (in Duns Scotus and Spinoza) versus equivocity, eminence, and analogy (in Suárez and Descartes). As always, Deleuze's ideas about the history of philosophy are very suggestive, but, from the philological or historiographic point of view, not fully developed. For an explanation of the theory of the formal distinction in Duns Scotus, see Etienne Gilson, *La philosophie au Moyen Age*, pp. 599ff.

9. Alquié presents a definition of Spinozism as the synthesis of Cartesian science and mathematics with Renaissance naturalism.

10. Martial Gueroult presents a thorough history of this controversy. See *Spinoza*, vol. 1, pp. 50, 428-61. Gueroult clearly supports an objectivist interpretation.

11. According to Gueroult, Hegel's interpretation is "the inspiration of a whole line of commentators who, from the beginning of the nineteenth century to today, have continued to maintain a common interpretation" (I, 466). See also pp. 462-68.

12. See Vincent Descombes, *Modern French Philosophy*, for an analysis of the dominant lines of French philosophy during these years.

13. "Parallelism" is not Spinoza's term, but rather is introduced by Leibniz's interpretation. Many have contended that it is not appropriate to apply this term to Spinoza's thought. Sylvain Zac, for example, objects to the use of the term "parallelism" to describe the relation between the Spinozian attributes: "It is not a correspondence nor a parallelism between the mental and the physiological, neither a term-to-term correspondence nor a correspondence of the wholes" (*L'idée de vie* 96-97). Zac argues that the attributes are not parallel, but instead are substantially identical, viewed from different perspectives. For this reason, it is important that Deleuze not claim an equality of correspondence, but an equality of principle. Given this nuance, it is not clear that Zac's objection would adequately address Deleuze's interpretation.

14. Antonio Negri poses forcefully the problem of the attributes as a problem of organization (*The Savage Anomaly* 53ff.). The ontological order that they constitute presents a being that is preformed, an ideal construction. This is the reason, Negri argues, that the attributes must drop out of the discussion when Spinoza develops toward practical and political concerns. Deleuze, however, seems to be either unaware of, or unconcerned with, this problem.

15. We will see that, although Deleuze eloquently proposes this ontological parallelism, he fails to apply it to its fullest at a crucial point in the investigation, when practice emerges on the terrain of constitution.

16. Special difficulties are presented for my thesis by the reappearance of the attributes in Part V of the *Ethics*. Negri maintains that this reappearance is due to the fact that Spinoza drafted different sections of Part V during different periods, that Part V contains residues of the pantheistic utopia of Spinoza's early work (169ff.). My Deleuzian proposal suggests a different explanation. I would maintain that Spinoza's effort in Part V to rise from the second to the third type of knowledge, to rise to the idea of God, requires a new speculative moment, a return to the earlier mode of research. The return to Spinoza's *Forschung* brings with it all of its scientific instruments, including the attributes.

17. In *Spinoza's Theory of Truth*, Thomas Mark gives a thorough account of Anglo-American and analytic interpretations of Spinoza's epistemology. Mark explains that the traditional approach (Joachim, Stuart Hampshire, Alisdair MacIntyre, etc.) poses Spinoza against a correspondence theory of truth and in favor of a "coherence theory" where truth is defined as coherence within the orderly system that constitutes reality. Mark argues, however, that Spinoza is better situated in the much older epistemological tradition of truth as being: "If we wish to see Spinoza's theory of truth in its historical setting, we must contrast the correspondence view not with coherence, but rather with theories of 'truth of being' or 'truth of things': ontological truth" (85). According to Mark, this theory of ontological truth situates Spinoza in the Platonic tradition in line with Plotinus, Anselm, and St. Augustine. Deleuze's reading is consistent with Mark's to a certain point, but the crucial factor is that Mark does not recognize, as Deleuze does, the central relationship between truth and power. Once the question of truth becomes also a question of power, Spinoza's epistemology tends toward a practical epistemology. Therefore, Deleuze's reading situates Spinoza's "ontological truth" not in the Platonic, but the Nietzschean, tradition.

18. A given idea of a circle may be clear and distinct, but it remains inadequate unless it expresses the path of its own production. An adequate idea of a circle might, for example, involve the idea of a fixed radius rotated around a central point; it expresses its cause. A more important and complex example would be the idea of justice: An adequate idea of justice would have to express the means by which we would produce or construct such an idea; it would involve an entire genealogy of ideas that result in this idea.

19. "When a number of bodies . . . are so constrained by other bodies that they lie upon one another, or if they move . . . that they communicate their motions to each other in a certain fixed manner, we shall say that those bodies are united with one another and that they all together compose one body or Individual" (*Ethics* IIP13Def).

20. For an extended discussion of the Spinozian conception of the multitude, see Antonio Negri, *The Savage Anomaly* (187-90, 194-210).

Works Cited

Alquié, Ferdinand. *Nature et verité dans la philosophie de Spinoza*. Les cours de Sorbonne, Paris, 1958.

_____. *Servitude et liberté selon Spinoza*. Les cours de Sorbonne, Paris, 1959.

Althusser, Louis. *Essays in Self-Criticism*, translated by Grahame Lock. New Left Books, London, 1976.

_____. *For Marx*, translated by Ben Brewster. Vintage Books, New York, 1969.

_____. *Reading Capital*, translated by Ben Brewster. New Left Books, London, 1970.

Aristotle. *Metaphysics*, translated by Hippocrates Apostle. Indiana University Press, Bloomington, 1973.

Balestrini, Nanni. *Vogliamo tutto*. Feltrinelli, Milan, 1971.

Barthélemy-Madaule, Madeleine. "Lire Bergson." *Les études bergsoniennes*, no. 8, 1968, pp. 83-120.

Bergson, Henri. *Ecrits et paroles*, textes rassemblés par Rose-Marie Mossé-Bastide, vol. 3. Presses Universitaires de France, Paris, 1959.

_____. *La Pensée et le Mouvant*. Presses Universitaires de France, Paris, 1941.

Bianquis, Geneviève. "Nietzsche et la philosophie." *Bulletin de la société française d'études nietschéennes*, no. 2, 1963, p. 37.

Butler, Judith. *Subjects of Desire*. Columbia University Press, New York, 1987.

Châtelet, François. *Hegel*. Seuil, Paris, 1968.

Deleuze, Gilles. "Bergson." *Les philosophes célèbres*, edited by Maurice Merleau-Ponty. Editions d'Art Lucien Mazenod, Paris, 1956, pp. 292-99.

_____. *Bergsonism*, translated by Hugh Tomlinson and Barbara Habberjam. Zone Books, New York, 1988.

_____. "La conception de la différence chez Bergson." *Les études bergsoniennes*, no. 4, 1956, pp. 77-112.

_____. "Le devenir révolutionnaire et les créations politiques." *Futur Antérieur*, no. 1, Spring 1990.

——. *Dialogues*, with Claire Parnet, translated by Hugh Tomlinson and Barbara Habberjam. Columbia University Press, New York, 1987.

——. *Différence et répétition*. Presses Universitaires de France, Paris, 1968.

——. "Du Christ à la bourgeoisie." *Espace*, 1946, pp. 93-106.

——. *Empiricism and Subjectivity*, translated by Constantin Boundas. Columbia University Press, New York, 1991.

——. *Expressionism in Philosophy: Spinoza*, translated by Martin Joughin. Zone Books, New York, 1990.

——. *Foucault*, translated by Seán Hand. University of Minnesota Press, Minneapolis, 1988.

——. *Instincts et institutions. Textes et documents philosophiques*. Hachette, Paris, 1953.

——. "Intellectuals and Power," with Michel Foucault. In Michel Foucault, *Language, Counter-Memory, Practice*. Cornell University Press, Ithaca, N.Y., 1977.

——. "Lettre à Michel Cressole." In Michel Cressole, *Deleuze*. Editions Universitaires, Paris, 1973.

——. *The Logic of Sense*, translated by Mark Lester with Charles Stivale. Columbia University Press, New York, 1990.

——. *Mémoire et vie: textes choisis*. Henri Bergson. Presses Universitaires de France, Paris, 1957.

——. "La méthode de dramatisation." *Bulletin de la société française de philosophie*, 28 January 1967, pp. 90-118.

——. "Mystère d'Ariane." *Bulletin de la société française d'études nietzschéennes*, no. 2, March 1963, pp. 12-15.

——. *Nietzsche and Philosophy*, translated by Hugh Tomlinson. Columbia University Press, New York, 1983.

——. "Signes et événements." *Magazine Littéraire*, no. 257, September 1988, pp. 16-25.

——. "Spinoza et la méthode générale de M. Guéroult." *Revue de métaphysique et de morale*, no. 4, 1969, pp. 426-37.

——. *Spinoza: Practical Philosophy*, translated by Robert Hurley. City Lights Books, San Francisco, 1988.

Deleuze, Gilles, and Félix Guattari. *A Thousand Plateaus*, translated by Brian Massumi. University of Minnesota Press, Minneapolis, 1987.

Descartes, René. *Discours de la méthode*, edited by Etienne Gilson. Vrin, Paris, 1925.

Descombes, Vincent. *Modern French Philosophy*, translated by L. Scott-Fox and J. M. Harding. Cambridge University Press, Cambridge, 1980.

Duns Scotus. *Philosophical Writings*, translated by Allan Wolter. Nelson, New York, 1962.

Gilson, Etienne. *La philosophie au Moyen Age*. Payot, Paris, 1986.

Grumley, John. *History and Totality: Radical Historicism from Hegel to Foucault*. Routledge, New York, 1989.

Gueroult, Martial. *Spinoza: Dieu (Ethique 1)*. Aubier-Montaigne, Paris, 1968.

Hardt, Michael. "The Anatomy of power." Foreword to Antonio Negri, *The Savage Anomaly*. University of Minnesota Press, Minneapolis, 1991, pp. xi-xvi.

——. "La renaissance hégélienne américaine et l'intériorisation du conflit." *Futur Antérieur*, no. 2, Spring 1990, pp. 133-46.

Hegel, G. W. F. *Lectures on the History of Philosophy*, translated by E. S. Haldane and Frances Simson. Routledge & Kegan Paul, London, 1968.

——. *Phenomenology of Spirit*, translated by A. V. Miller. Oxford University Press, Oxford, 1977.

——. *Science of Logic*, translated by A. V. Miller. Humanities Press, Atlantic Highlands, N.J., 1969.

Houlgate, Stephen. *Hegel, Nietzsche and the Criticism of Metaphysics*. Cambridge University Press, Cambridge, 1986.

Klossowski, Pierre. *Nietzsche et le cercle vicieux*. Mercure de France, Paris, 1969.

Kojève, Alexandre. *Introduction to the Reading of Hegel*, translated by James Nichols, Jr. Basic Books, New York, 1969.

Macherey, Pierre. *Hegel ou Spinoza*. Maspero, Paris, 1979.

Marcuse, Herbert. *Reason and Revolution: Hegel and the Rise of Social Theory*. Beacon Press, Boston, 1960.

Mark, Thomas. *Spinoza's Theory of Truth*. Columbia University Press, New York, 1972.

Marx, Karl. *Capital*, vol. 1, translated by Ben Fowkes. Vintage Books, New York, 1977.

———. "Critique of Hegel's Philosophy of Right." *The Marx-Engels Reader*, edited by Robert Tucker. Norton, New York, 1978.

Massumi, Brian. "Pleasures of Philosophy." Foreword to *A Thousand Plateaus* by Deleuze and Guattari. University of Minnesota Press, Minneapolis, 1987.

Mossé-Bastide, Rose-Marie. "Bergson et Spinoza." *Revue de métaphysique et de morale*, 1949, pp. 67-82.

Negri, Antonio. *La fabbrica della strategia: 33 lezioni su Lenin* (1972). CLEUP and Libri Rossi, Padua, 1976.

———. *The Savage Anomaly: The Power of Spinoza's Metaphysics and Politics*. University of Minnesota Press, Minneapolis, 1991.

Nietzsche, Friedrich. *The Portable Nietzsche*, edited and translated by Walter Kaufmann. Penguin Books, New York, 1954.

———. *Twilight of the Idols*, translated by R. J. Hollingdale. Penguin Books, New York, 1968.

Ockham, William. *Philosophical Writings*, edited by P. Boehner. Nelson, New York, 1957.

Rose, Gillian. "The New Bergsonism." *Dialectic of Nihilism*. Basil Blackwell, New York, 1984, pp. 87-108.

Roth, Michael. *Knowing and History: Appropriations of Hegel in Twentieth-Century France*. Cornell University Press, Ithaca, N.Y., 1988.

Spinoza, Baruch. *Complete Works*, vol. 1, edited and translated by Edwin Curley. Princeton University Press, Princeton, 1985.

———. *Opera*, edited by Carl Gebhardt. 4 vols. Carl Winter, Heidelberg, 1925.

Suárez, Francisco. *Disputaciones metafísicas*. 4 vols. Editorial Gredos, Madrid, 1960.

Taylor, Charles. *Hegel*. Cambridge University Press, Cambridge, 1975.

Tronti, Mario. *Operai e capitale*. Einaudi, Turin, 1966.

Wahl, Jean. "Nietzsche et la philosophie." *Revue de métaphysique et de morale*, no. 3, 1963, pp. 352-79.

Zac, Sylvain. *La morale de Spinoza*. Presses Universitaires de France, Paris, 1959.

———. "Les thèmes spinozistes dans la philosophie de Bergson." *Les études bergsoniennes*, no. 8, 1968, pp. 121-58.

———. *L'idée de vie dans la philosophie de Spinoza*. Presses Universitaires de France, Paris, 1963.

Index

Scholastics, 126 n. 11; on causality, 5-9, 114,
125 nn. 2, 4; on critique, xiii, 50; on
univocity, 20; on the virtual, 17. *See also*
Ockham, William; Duns Scotus
singularity, 10-11, 59-63, 67-70, 90, 112-14
speculation, ontological, 66, 69-71, 77-79,
112-15; as distinct from practice, 58-59,
87, 95-96. *See also* affirmation
Spinoza, Baruch, 56-59, 125 n. 4; the
attributes and parallelism, 74-76, 79-87;
common notions, 95-100, 118;
epistemology, 87-91, 100-104; power to
exist and power to be affected, 71-73,
91-95, 118; singularity, 59-63, 67-68, 113;
social organization, 108-111, 121;
univocal expression, 63-66, 68-70, 80-82,
113-14. *See also* Bergson, Henri:

interpretation of Spinoza; Hegel, G. W. F.:
interpretation of Spinoza; Nietzsche,
Friedrich: in relation to Spinoza
Suárez, Francisco, 125 n. 2, 130 n. 8

Taylor, Charles, 3, 40-43
Tronti, Mario, 44, 128 n. 5, 129 n. 12

univocity, 20, 24-25, 63-66, 68-70, 80-82,
113-14

virtual, 14-19, 20-21, 63. *See also* actual

Wahl, Jean, 33, 38-39, 128 n. 6, 129 n. 14
work, 39-46. *See also* Hegel, G. W. F.:
master and slave dialectic

Zac, Sylvain, 84, 130 nn. 3, 6, 131 n. 13

Michael Hardt is the translator of Antonio Negri's *Savage Anomaly: The Power of Spinoza's Metaphysics and Politics* (Minnesota, 1990) and Giorgio Agamben's *The Coming Community* (Minnesota, 1993). The University of Minnesota Press will also publish his forthcoming book, coauthored with Negri, *Labor of Dionysus: Communism as Critique of the Capitalist and Socialist State-form.*